INSIDE

DISAPPOINTMENT

CWR

WAVERLEY ABBEY INSIGHT SERIES

INSIGHT INTO

DISAPPOINTMENT

Chris Ledger and Chris Orme

CWR

Copyright © 2014 CWR

Published 2015 by CWR, Waverley Abbey House, Waverley Lane, Farnham, Surrey GU9 8EP UK. Registered Charity No. 294387. Registered Limited Company No. 1990308.

The right of Chris Ledger and Chris Orme to be identified as the authors of this work has been asserted by them in accordance with the Copyright, Designs and Patents Act 1988, sections 77 and 78.

For list of National Distributors visit www.cwr.org.uk/distributors

Unless otherwise indicated, all Scripture references are from the Holy Bible: New International Version (NIVUK), copyright © 1973, 1978, 1984, 2011 by the International Bible Society. Other versions used: The Message: Scripture taken from THE MESSAGE. Copyright © 1993, 1994, 1995, 1996, 2000, 2001, 2002. Used by permission of NavPress Publishing Group. TLB: The Living Bible, copyright © 1971, by Tyndale House Foundation. All rights reserved. NLT: Scripture quotations marked (NLT) are taken from the Holy Bible, New Living Translation, copyright © 1996, 2004, 2007, 2013 by Tyndale House Foundation. Used by permission of Tyndale House Publishers, Inc., Carol Stream, Illinois 60188. All rights reserved. NKJV: Scripture taken from the New King James Version®. Copyright © 1982 by Thomas Nelson, Inc. Used by permission. All rights reserved.

Every effort has been made to ensure that this book contains the correct permissions and references, but if anything has been inadvertently overlooked the Publisher will be pleased to make the necessary arrangements at the first opportunity. Please contact the Publisher directly.

Concept development, editing, design and production by CWR.

Printed in the UK by Page Bros.

ISBN: 978-1-78259-272-3

WAVERLEY ABBEY
INSIGHT SERIES

The *Waverley Abbey Insight Series* has been developed in response to the great need to help people understand and face some key issues that many of us struggle with today. CWR's ministry spans teaching, training and publishing, and this series draws on all of these areas of ministry.

Sourced from material first presented over Insight Days by CWR at their base, Waverley Abbey House, presenters and authors have worked in close co-operation to bring this series together, offering clear insight, teaching and help on a broad range of subjects and issues. Bringing biblical understanding and godly insight, these books are written both for those who help others and those who face these issues themselves.

CONTENTS

INTRODUCTION

'Life is not about waiting for the storms to pass … it's about learning to dance in the rain.'

(Anonymous)

Life is never problem free and disappointment affects us all to varying degrees. Being a Christian certainly isn't some kind of insurance policy against bad things happening to us. Jesus Himself warned, 'I have told you these things, so that in me you may have peace. In this world you will have trouble. But take heart! I have overcome the world' (John 16:33). We believe God is more interested in refining our characters than He is in our being comfortable! But how do we cope and move on through bitter disappointments? How do we trust a God who may seem to have 'let us down'? These questions and many more like them are why we wrote this book.

We have been close friends for almost thirty years and this is the second *Insight* book we have co-authored. Like others in the *Insight* series, it has been developed from the original seminar on the subject, which Chris (Ledger) presented at Waverley Abbey House. *Insight into Disappointment* has been born of our personal experiences as much as from our intellectual understanding of the subject.

I (Chris Orme) lost almost all my hearing virtually overnight twenty-eight years ago when my youngest daughter was a year old, so spent most of my children's growing years battling with the frustrations and disappointments that profound and incurable deafness brings. A cochlear implant two years ago has made a huge difference, but I am still living with the effects and disappointments of being deaf.

My (Chris Ledger's) dream of having a healthy daughter was shattered twenty-four years ago when my elder daughter, Julia, became ill with Chronic Fatigue Syndrome/Myalgic Encephalomyelitis. Julia has been more or less housebound since then and for many years bedbound as well, lacking the energy even to speak. So for me there have been numerous heartaches and disappointments along the road, but also many blessings, as I have come to appreciate the little things when the big things become impossible.

It's been a privilege to co-author this book because the theme resonates with us on an emotional, as well as a spiritual and theoretical, level. Our prayer is that whatever the nature of their disappointment, this book will help readers, and those who are reading to help others, to acknowledge what is going on in their lives, understand the journey of coming to terms with a shattered dream, and to work through this to a place where new hope can be found.

Chris Ledger and Chris Orme, 2014

CHAPTER ONE

AN INTRODUCTION TO DISAPPOINTMENT

'… And they lived happily ever after.'

As small children, that's the way we like – and expect – fairy stories to end. The challenges have been faced, the dangers are past and the 'baddies' vanquished. The prince has won his princess, true love has triumphed and … they lived happily ever after.

Naturally, as we grow older, wiser and perhaps slightly more pessimistic, we come to realise that, for most of us, life isn't like that. At some point in our lives almost all of us will face bitter disappointment in one area or another. Hopes and dreams lie shattered at our feet. Take childhood dreams for instance. What were yours? Have any been fulfilled? Are there any that, painfully, have not been realised? Perhaps you can relate to the following example.

A nine-year-old girl is doing really well at ballet. Her dance teacher puts her forward for an audition to work with a real ballet troupe and perform in one of their productions. She practises and practises; she dreams of dancing in that production. Then the day of the audition arrives and she's not feeling very well. She doesn't dance to her usual standard and her name isn't read out. She is bitterly disappointed. 'Never mind,' say her mum and her teacher, 'You can try again next year.' *Next* year... a whole year to wait? That's an eternity to a nine-year-old! 'Hope deferred makes the heart sick,' says Proverbs 13:12. She cries bitterly all the way home, her dream shattered.

Ballet might not have been your thing. Perhaps your dream was to play for your favourite football team but this dream came to nothing, despite your greatest efforts, like turning up to every practice. Or perhaps your dream was of a happy marriage. From your early teens you imagined the kind of person you would marry, the thrill of falling in love, the joy of your wedding day and the utter release and peace of being held by someone who loved you above all others. But it hasn't happened.

There are countless other 'disappointment' scenarios, where cherished childhood hopes and dreams don't work out as we had desired and anticipated. Then there are those dreams we develop later. Maybe on reaching your mid-forties you pause to step back and take stock of your career life so far and what you hope to accomplish in the future. After due thought, you make a conscious decision to stay with the firm and give it your best shot. Then, five years later, after hundreds of late nights, long weekends and working during your holidays, you're passed over for promotion. Your dream job crumbles into dust and ashes.

You have doubtless met people who have seen their dreams shattered: the couple who would have made wonderful parents, but hopes for children have been dashed after repeated miscarriages; the young person whose career in law has to be abandoned because of clinical depression; the man convinced of God's call to ordained ministry who is turned down by the selection committee; the mother (whose testimony we'll share later in the book) whose only child, a 'miracle baby' according to doctors, died of cancer before she was forty. The authors of this book have encountered all these situations and more. None of us has to look far to find others who are living with huge disappointments and shattered dreams.

These losses may be in the area of our emotions, our finances, our health – even our spiritual life – but however they manifest themselves, disappointment engulfs us. We may feel despairing, disillusioned, dejected. Worse still, we may feel as though God has abandoned us or is trying to punish us. One woman who certainly felt like this was Naomi. Let's look at her biblical example of a journey through disappointment.

A biblical example of disappointment – Naomi's journey

The book of Ruth in the Old Testament, although primarily about the young woman of the title, is set against the shattered dreams of an older woman – her mother-in-law, Naomi. Naomi's story illustrates both the pain of dashed hopes and shattered dreams and the process through which Naomi went as a result. Her story teaches us that while our dreams of good things may shatter, our pain will always have a purpose, such as:

- to help us to become more God-dependent than self-dependent;
- to help us to discover true hope;
- to open the door to new dreams.

Let's trace Naomi's journey from shattered dreams and despair to hope and a new beginning. The first five verses of the first chapter of Ruth describe a catalogue of disasters that leave Naomi's hopes and dreams in tatters. We learn that Naomi, her husband and their two sons leave their home and their extended family in Bethlehem because of a famine there. They travel to foreign territory (nearby Moab) expecting to stay there just until the famine is over.

Things don't work out as they'd anticipated. Shortly after their arrival in Moab, Naomi's first dream is shattered when her husband dies. However, her sons marry Moabite women, and with two new daughters-in-law, Naomi perhaps allowed herself to dream once more, this time of grandchildren. But another tragedy occurs. Both her sons die, childless, so once again her hopes are dashed – the twin hopes of grandchildren and that her sons would care and provide for her in her old age.

God seemed to do nothing to preserve Naomi's hopes – the hopes she thought were essential to her happiness. He appeared to have snatched away her dream of growing old with a devoted husband, of seeing her sons and their wives in a loving relationship and of grandchildren. God could have allowed Naomi to experience all those blessings, none of which was an unrealistic expectation. But God didn't allow them. What was the result? Despair set in.

Four characteristics of despair:
1. Emotions of sadness and loss
2. A feeling of abandonment
3. A sense of bitterness
4. Hopelessness

Any or all of these characteristics may be part of our own journey as we seek to come to terms with disappointment and shattered dreams. Look at Naomi's analysis of her situation in Ruth 1:8–12. Her sense of abandonment shows. Naomi believed that her daughters-in-law would be better off spending time with anyone other than herself. We can feel like this too: *there's something wrong with me; life has abandoned me; you go and join the crowd.*

Then in verse 13, Naomi confirms her bitterness: 'It is more bitter for me than for you, because the LORD's hand has turned against me!' Here is the measure of her desolation: Naomi feels that God is against her, that He has punished her by taking her husband and sons and abandoned her in an alien land.

One daughter-in-law heeds Naomi's words and returns to her former home, but Ruth refuses to leave, clinging to Naomi like a limpet. They arrive back in Bethlehem, the older woman so changed that people are not quite sure that it really is Naomi. She greets her old friends with: 'Don't call me Naomi' (which means 'pleasant') and tells them to: 'Call me Mara' (which means 'bitter'), 'because the Almighty has made my life very bitter' (Ruth 1:20).

Naomi lost no time in revealing her bitterness to these old friends. It's clear that she sincerely believed that she would never know true happiness again. But not only did Naomi feel an utter loss of hope of any return to earlier blessings that had brought joy and security, she believed that the tragedies that had befallen her were God's doing: 'I went away full, but the LORD has brought me back empty ... The LORD has afflicted me; the Almighty has brought misfortune upon me' (Ruth 1:21). She was plainly saying: 'I have nothing left and it's all God's doing.'

So, at the end of this first chapter we see a sad, bitter, empty woman – her happiness destroyed, her hopes shattered; her dreams unfulfilled. But, despite all appearances to the contrary, God had *not* abandoned Naomi. He was planning to give her a new dream, renewed hope and a deep and lasting joy. The catalyst was her daughter-in-law, Ruth.

When we are in despair because we have hit rock bottom, deliverance often comes through another person. In Naomi's case, that person was Ruth. Ruth asked her depressed and inactive mother-in-law for permission to 'go to the fields and pick up the leftover grain' (Ruth 2:2). (This activity, known as 'gleaning' was part of the provision for the poor and needy, enshrined in the Law of Moses.) And 'As it turned out, she was working in a field belonging to Boaz' (Ruth 2:3). Boaz just so happened to be one of Naomi's wealthy relatives and if he were to marry Ruth, both Ruth's and Naomi's financial troubles would be over. There were obstacles to overcome and plenty of patience to be practised, but Boaz did indeed marry Ruth and 'the LORD enabled her to conceive' (Ruth 4:13) their son, Obed.

Naomi's dreams of growing old with her husband and enjoying her sons as adults were gone but God had put something new and wonderful into her life. She was blessed with a devoted daughter-in-law, 'better to you than seven sons' (Ruth 4:15), which was the highest accolade the community could offer because Israelites regarded seven sons as the perfect family. The women of the town announced, 'Naomi has a son' (Ruth 4:17) because Obed would be reckoned as her husband's son, so Naomi is no longer regarded as childless. The story ends with the amazing fact that this baby was the grandfather of Jesse, the father of King David and therefore an ancestor of Jesus.

This biblical example shows us that shattered dreams skew

our vision. Naomi's assessment of her situation on her return to Bethlehem was by no means the whole picture! In fact she ends up a deeply contented woman, aware that sometimes God has a higher purpose for our lives than merely for things to go well from a human perspective. In her old age, Naomi experienced a joy that more than replaced the happiness she had lost. God had indeed, through Ruth and Boaz, given her 'beauty instead of ashes, the oil of joy instead of mourning, and a garment of praise instead of a spirit of despair' (Isa. 61:3). It's important to note that this transformation didn't come about overnight. It took time. It was a process; a journey.

THE FIVE STAGES OF THE DISAPPOINTMENT JOURNEY

If we picture life as a journey, we might describe disappointment as an unwanted and unscheduled stop on that journey. For Naomi it was tragedy, but whatever the cause, life comes to a standstill; our vehicle has broken down. Then we splutter forward along a road with new twists and turns. This book uses this metaphor to enable us to see the stages of working through our shattered dreams as these five stages (see Appendix):

1. **The Lay By** is our first stop. We pull in, shocked and in disbelief, to assess and acknowledge the impact disappointment has had on us and the damage it has caused.

2. We move on to **Despair Street**. This involves a sense of loss and despair. We try to make sense of the confusion we're experiencing. We ask God, 'Why?'

3. Then we hit **the Bumpy Track**. We can experience a range of crippling thoughts and emotions because of our expectations and unmet goals.

4. Next we reach **Struggle Lane**, a lonely place where we feel there is nothing more to do but give up. This is the crucial stage where we can choose to surrender our struggles to God.

5. Finally, we find ourselves climbing up **Hope Avenue.** We accept what has happened, we experience a time of healing and we find a new hope.

We realise, of course, that some of you reading this may already have started on this journey; you may be experiencing any one of these stages right now. Wherever you are, our prayer is that this book will help you to:

- identify the impact that disappointment, loss and shattered dreams have had on your life;
- come to terms with that impact;
- find new strength and hope in God amidst the disappointment.

You may find the most helpful way to use this book is to read it through in its entirety once and then read certain sections in more detail as you move on in the journey. Others reading this may do so because they are seeking to come alongside someone struggling with disappointment, and we hope that you will find these insights helpful too.

REFLECTION

Like Naomi, when we are struggling to come to terms with loss or disappointment, we may feel as though God has abandoned us, or is punishing us and yet, deep down, we still cling to the truths of our faith. At such times it can be helpful to turn to Scripture for comfort.

Reflect on the following passages:

Deep calls to deep
in the roar of your waterfalls;
all your waves and breakers
have swept over me.

By day the LORD directs his love,
at night his song is with me –
a prayer to the God of my life.
I say to God my Rock,
'Why have you forgotten me?
Why must I go about mourning,
oppressed by the enemy?'
My bones suffer mortal agony
as my foes taunt me,
saying to me all day long,
'Where is your God?'

Why, my soul, are you downcast?
Why so disturbed within me?
Put your hope in God,
for I will yet praise him,
my Saviour and my God.
(Psa. 42:7–11)

When you pass through the waters,
I will be with you;
and when you pass through the rivers,
they will not sweep over you.
When you walk through the fire,
you will not be burned;
the flames will not set you ablaze.
For I am the LORD your God,
the Holy One of Israel, your Saviour
(Isa. 43:2–3)

ACTIVITY
Consider whether there are any aspects of Naomi's story with which you can identify.

PRAYER
Thank You, Lord, that I don't have to explain to You how I'm feeling and why, because You know all about it and all about me. Help me to know that You are the same loving and compassionate Father, whatever my struggle may be and however I feel. Help me to trust that You will walk beside me in my journey through disappointment and loss. Amen.

CHAPTER TWO

THE LAY BY

**ACKNOWLEDGING DISAPPOINTMENT AND
ASSESSING THE IMPACT OF SHATTERED DREAMS**

Disappointment is the antithesis of hope. And the stark truth is that we will all face disappointments in different areas and at different stages of our lives: people will disappoint us; situations and events will disappoint us. Some disappointments are more acute than others; some occur as one-off, major events in our lives. The following is not an exhaustive list, but we may experience disappointment through:

- the death of a loved one, particularly if that death was unexpected, tragic or untimely;
- being made redundant or passed over for promotion;
- a relationship that has broken down or hasn't worked out as we had hoped;
- having trouble conceiving a longed-for baby;
- a beloved child going off the rails, suffering a long-term

illness or not being able to hold down a job after working hard to get the necessary qualifications;

- a promise of God seemingly not being fulfilled.

Listen to some ways in which people describe the disappointment they felt when a dream was shattered or their hopes dashed. Perhaps you can identify with one or more of them:

- 'It feels as though someone kicked me in the stomach. I've got my breath back now but all I can do is cry.'
- 'I can't go on like this; I wish I were dead.'
- 'How can I bear this pain?'
- 'Right now I have no hope of ever being happy again.'
- 'I feel my heart is broken – fractured. Will it ever mend?'

LOSS

In any disappointment there will always be an area of **loss**: something has been taken away or an expectation has not been met. This results in **grief** and includes **mourning** and/ or **struggling**, which is what we do in order to come to terms with the disappointment. Here's an example of loss from author Chris Orme's experience:

Whilst still in my thirties, and with my four daughters aged eleven months, five, nine and eleven, I lost virtually all my hearing, more or less overnight. During the weeks and months of tests and diagnoses that ensued, I was grief-stricken. I felt totally out of control, frightened and bewildered about how I would manage. I was concerned about what effects the onset of deafness would have on my relationships with my husband and children. I

> was desperately worried about how the children would cope with having a deafened mother. My social life disappeared – I couldn't even talk to other mothers in the playground, let alone face a room full of people in a social situation. It was an appallingly difficult time and in the end my youngest child had to go to nursery full-time because she couldn't cope with not being able to be understood by her mother. It was like a nightmare from which I couldn't wake up.

Being human means suffering loss and disappointment. Some losses and disappointments are reversible, like a broken limb that gradually mends, but catastrophic loss is like having a limb amputated; each new day forces us to confront the impact of that loss.

Loss can do its damage instantly, like the destruction a tsunami wreaks, sweeping away everything in its path. Or it can do damage gradually, like a river swelling with incessant rain, then finally breaking its banks. Loss can leave the landscapes of our lives changed forever.

When disappointment hits us, whether it does so like a tidal wave or like a slow but steady overflowing of the river bank, it's important to identify the constants in our lives and to focus on the sources of stability and strength we have around us. These may be close family ties, long-held friendships, the church community, work friends etc. We need people with whom we can be real, people who will not judge us and who can be depended upon to be there for us during the difficult patches.

It's important to recognise that loss can affect every area of our lives and to know what these areas are. The following diagram shows these areas and how they can be affected by loss:

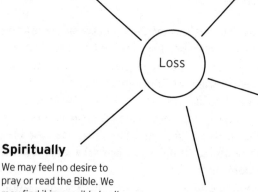

Socially

We may have no energy to invest in life because all our energy is directed towards processing the loss. There may be a desire to withdraw from normal social contacts and there may be no inclination to attend regular leisure activities because we feel we can no longer enjoy them.

Emotionally

Our emotions can be all over the place, causing us to feel completely drained; we may cry most of the time.

In the workplace

We may be unable to concentrate or stay focused on the task in hand.

Spiritually

We may feel no desire to pray or read the Bible. We may find it impossible to sit through a church service without weeping. We may lose all interest in spiritual things, feeling that God has forgotten or abandoned us.

Physically

Loss of energy means we may want to sleep all the time or, at the other extreme, we may find we are unable to sleep. Fatigue may mean we feel hungrier than usual or we may find ourselves 'comfort eating'. Conversely, we may be unable to eat. Other appetites may disappear, for example we may suffer a loss of libido.

Dealing with loss

There is no value in quantifying our losses or in comparing our personal disappointments with someone else's; it's not a competition to determine whose loss is the most traumatic. Loss is loss and disappointment is disappointment, whatever the circumstances. Pain is pain and it is entirely individual. No one else can really know the pain you are experiencing. No two losses are the same and they inflict a different kind of pain on each one of us. The most productive question to ask is not, 'Whose pain is worse?' but 'What insights can I gain from this disappointment and how can I grow through it?'

Spiritual growth involves the *choices* we make, the *grace* we receive and the *transformation* we experience as we come to terms with our shattered dreams.

Start by *choosing*, however falteringly, to turn towards the disappointment (see the Activity), then yield to the loss and start processing the pain. Remember: it's a journey.

REFLECTION

Job has just received a succession of messages telling him that he has lost everything – his livestock, his servants and his children. What does he do? 'Job ... fell to the ground in worship and said: "Naked I came from my mother's womb, and naked I shall depart. The LORD gave and the LORD has taken away; may the name of the LORD be praised"' (Job 1:20–21).

King David pleaded with God for his child by Bathsheba to live, fasting and spending the nights lying on the ground. On the seventh day the child died. What does David do? 'David got up ... went into the house of the LORD and worshipped' (2 Sam. 12:20).

ACTIVITY

Give yourself half an hour, or as long as you need, to identify the impact of your loss, your disappointment, your shattered dreams, on the different areas of your life – and, if appropriate, on the lives of your family. It's easier to make progress and move on from something that you've identified than it is to move on from a vague 'mass' of lost dreams and hopes.

PRAYER

Lord, as I start this journey of working through my loss and coming to terms with the disappointment in my life, I ask that I may be conscious that You are accompanying me, wanting to come alongside me, willing to enter into the pain and grief I'm feeling. Hold on to me; don't let me go. Amen.

CHAPTER THREE

DESPAIR STREET

Having assessed the damage resulting from our disappointment and shattered hopes, we understand the need to move on. We pull away from the Lay By, with perhaps some choking and spluttering, and find ourselves lost in Despair Street. It's not a pleasant place to be but others have been there before us.

A New Testament case study: The road to Emmaus (Luke 24:13–35)
Luke is the only one of the Gospel writers who tells, in detail, this story of a meeting with the risen Christ on the road to Emmaus. Both travellers were followers of Jesus although they weren't part of the inner group of disciples known as 'the Twelve'. One of them is called Cleopas but we are told neither the name nor the gender of the second person; however it's possible that they were a married couple returning to their home, bewildered and despairing after the events that had culminated in the crucifixion. As they walked, they were discussing all that had happened (v14), trying to make sense of it. These were ordinary people whose hopes had been shattered.

In a culture where people travel together for company and protection, they are joined by someone they don't recognise, who asks them what they are talking about (v17). They are amazed that He could even ask the question (v18) and their detailed reply (vv19–21) indicates their bitter disappointment: 'we *had hoped* that he was the one who was going to redeem Israel' (emphasis added). Their hopes were dashed. Life seemed bleak and empty.

These two people were actually quite privileged from a spiritual point of view. They were Jews living in Israel, so they had a background of faith: they knew the Old Testament scriptures, the promise of a Messiah and they had begun to believe and hope that Jesus, 'a prophet, powerful in word and deed' (v19) was the fulfilment of that promise. Then came the awful events of the crucifixion. They had heard reports of the empty tomb from eye-witnesses (vv22–24), but these had neither convinced nor encouraged them. And yet … here was none other than Jesus Himself, walking incognito with them down Despair Street.

We can perhaps identify with them in some ways. Luke tells us that they were 'kept from recognising him' (v16), and when we find ourselves lost in Despair Street we may find that we have 'lost' God and ask, 'Where is God in all of this?' Jesus gives them (and us) permission to pour out their hearts, to talk about what is going on. Facts often come before expressions of feelings about those facts. Jesus didn't ask, 'How do you feel?' but 'What is going on?' Their reply indicates how long they had been wandering in Despair Street, 'And what is more, it is the third day since all this took place' (v21). Three days on and they were still trying to make some kind of sense of the tragedy.

Proverbs 13:12 tells us: 'Hope deferred makes the heart sick, but a longing fulfilled is a tree of life.' Time does not always heal. Sometimes it makes things worse. There are telling details in Luke's account here, details that give psychological verity to the story. In verse 17, after Jesus asks them what they're talking about, Luke records that they 'stood still, their faces downcast'. They are immobilised by loss of hope; their paralysed faces say it all – 'downcast'. Emotionally they are on edge; their answer (v18) is verging on the snappy.

These two disciples were well and truly lost in Despair Street – despairing, discouraged, disappointed. As we pull away from the Lay By where we've made a preliminary assessment of the damage that our particular disappointment has caused, we, too, may well find ourselves there.

ASKING 'WHY?'

It is almost inevitable that, once the initial shock and grief begin to subside, we find ourselves asking, 'Why?' In the circumstances of loss, that 'why' has two dimensions – we turn, bewildered and despairing, to God and ask, 'Why, God?' That question is a general one, a cry that echoes down the years from all those confronted with suffering, pain and evil. How do we square what we are experiencing with our belief in and experience of an all-powerful God of love? The second dimension is personal – about ourselves: 'Why me?' And that question too, has many ramifications.

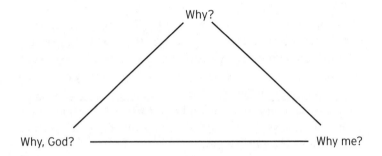

We ask why for a number of reasons; the two most relevant here are:

- We feel, both instinctively and from experience, that there is an order about the world and about life that makes sense. If that order disappears, we feel insecure.
- If something goes wrong we seek to know the reason for it, so that we can perhaps prevent it happening again.

Here is Chris Ledger's personal experience of this:

> That small three-letter word 'why?' poses a question that people have wrestled with for years – and I am no different. I agonised over it for a whole twelve months when my eldest daughter was first confined to bed with a chronic illness; her life at university had suddenly come to a full stop and my life was turned upside down as I adjusted to caring for her. I wanted to find a logical answer to why this had happened. I thought that if I could answer this question, I could learn from it; the illness would then make more sense and I would feel more secure about

life because I would have a reason for why the suffering had hit her. As I wrestled with trying to find an answer, it was like *101 Dalmatians* – I would come up with over a hundred reasons, for none of which there was evidence! This searching and wrestling caused me a lot of internal tension. Finally after about a year, I suddenly decided that my searching was no use: *there was no rational answer*, so it was a waste of time to ask. It was time to let it go ... and wow! What a difference it made. In accepting the mystery of life and illness, I felt much more at peace.

WHY ME?

When faced with disappointment, our first question may be, 'Why has this happened?' But what we probably mean is, 'Why has this happened *to me*?' 'What have I done to deserve this?' 'Am I being punished?' Initially we are most likely to ask these questions to ourselves and we answer them ourselves, but sometimes the responses we come up with only make us feel worse:

- Perhaps God doesn't love me.
- Perhaps God isn't as powerful as we think He is.
- Perhaps God doesn't exist.
- Perhaps I'm not good enough.
- Perhaps I'm to blame.
- Perhaps I'm being punished.

The last three responses in particular can be very unhelpful, even destructive. In pondering the possibilities of 'I'm not good enough', 'I'm to blame' ('It's all my fault') or 'I'm being punished', we can start having nagging thoughts that *we* have caused this tragedy or illness by some action or inaction on our part. This so

31

easily leads to guilt, which can gnaw away at us for years and can lead to self-criticism, self-hatred and destructive behaviour. All these simply add to the burden of our disappointment and loss. Here's Chris Ledger's experience of this:

> In coming to terms with the disappointment, loss and the shattered dreams of my sick daughter's future, I prayed against that 'hardening of the heart' that is mentioned so often in the Bible. I asked God to keep my heart tender, praying that I wouldn't allow any irrational guilt to niggle away at me. In no way was I to blame. With the passing of years and my daughter still very ill, I remember how I was ironing one day when the thought popped into my mind, 'Well, you must have done something really wrong for God not to hear and answer your prayers for your daughter', and I became aware of my tummy doing somersaults as guilt enticed me to beckon it into my life and make it welcome. It took a lot of determination to remind myself that I could choose *not* to believe this taunting voice that wanted me to feel bad about myself, so in God's strength I resisted, and soon felt at peace again.

There is a widely-held, if largely unspoken, belief that people should 'get what they deserve' because God causes good or bad things to happen to us according to our deeds. There is an element of truth in this, because the Bible teaches, 'Do not be deceived: God cannot be mocked. A man reaps what he sows' (Gal. 6:7). To give two very simple examples: if we persist for years and years in smoking sixty cigarettes a day, then getting cancer is likely to be the result, or if we fall into behaviour that is contrary to

God's ways, such as alcohol abuse, the ramifications may be the physical condition of cirrhosis. However, this is a *consequence* of sin, not a *punishment* for it. That verse in Galatians doesn't mean that if life goes well for someone they are blameless and if they are hit by tragedy they have done something awful and the tragedy is the punishment. That is most emphatically not a Christian belief.

An Old Testament case study: Job

Job, whose catalogue of terrible sufferings is described in the Old Testament book that bears his name, went directly to God with his frequent 'Why?' questions.

- 'Why have you made me your target?' (Job 7:20)
- 'Why do you hide your face ...?' (13:24)
- Why 'should I struggle in vain?' (9:29)
- 'Why does the Almighty not set times for judgment?' (24:1)
- 'Why then did you bring me out of the womb?' (10:18)

Job had lost his home, his family, his wealth and his health because God had given Satan permission to test him. Having lost everything, he ended up covered from head to toe in boils and sitting on an ash heap. When his friends saw his condition, they were so shocked that they were speechless for seven days and nights (Job 2:12–13). Then Job shared his feelings with them. Even though God had declared Job to be blameless, they assaulted him in a cycle of attacks and defences.

Throughout the book, it is Job's friends who persist in the belief that Job's suffering must be deserved and they conclude that he needs to repent. Yet we are shown that none of Job's suffering is a punishment for his sins, and that all the losses, ill health and misfortune he suffers come not from God but from Satan. The book exposes the fallibility of the 'What have I done to deserve this?' line of thought, alongside the reality of deep and raw suffering and Job's sense of having been abandoned.

A New Testament case study: a man born blind (John 9:1–35)
In contrast to the Old Testament thinking revealed by Job's friends, in the New Testament Jesus rejects the idea that suffering, sickness or disability is a punishment for sin. In the story of the man born blind, whom Jesus healed, the disciples, reflecting those Old Testament views, ask Jesus, 'Rabbi, who sinned, this man or his parents, that he was born blind?' (v2). Jesus responded, 'Neither this man nor his parents sinned … but this happened so that the works of God might be displayed in him' (v3). Jesus' reply has helped many to be freed from the burden of believing that their physical suffering is some kind of punishment from God.

WHY, GOD?

We may find that having asked, 'Why has this happened to me?' we go beyond that very personal angle and ask questions similar to those that Job put to God, questions that are much wider and more general:

- Why is there suffering if there is a God of love?
- Why doesn't God put an end to all sickness, disease and life's traumas?
- Why does God permit the innocent to suffer pain, disappointment and shattered dreams?

The question, 'If God is all-loving and all-powerful, why doesn't He ...?' is voiced over and over again, whenever tragedy or loss affects us. It's a natural question, springing from the agony of our hearts. Our human reasoning is: If I loved someone and had the power to stop their suffering or to meet their needs, I would do it! Perhaps you can relate to the following. If God is all-loving and all-powerful:

- Why doesn't He cure my mother of Alzheimer's?
- Why doesn't He answer my prayers?
- Why doesn't He straighten out my rebellious kids?
- Why doesn't He heal my daughter?
- Why doesn't He give me the husband I desire?
- Why doesn't He give me the child I long for?

Struggling to depend on an apparently unresponsive God in the midst of shattered dreams and disappointment can be very tough on our faith, stretching it to the limit.

An Old Testament case study: The Israelites in Egypt (Exod. 1–2)

The Israelites arrived in Egypt when Joseph, who had been sold into slavery there by his jealous older brothers, invited his entire family to come and live there to escape famine in their home country. For generations they flourished and multiplied there until a new king who did not know Joseph (Exod. 1:8) came to the throne, and enslaved the Israelites who were perceived as a threat.

Oppression increased over the years and the Israelites would most probably have asked the same sort of questions about God and suffering as we have outlined above. Enslaved as they were, they must often have felt close to despair as God seemed to hide His face – uncaring, distant, silent; unfair. He did not immediately set about delivering His people and the escalating harshness they suffered appears to discredit all that Scripture has to say about a concerned and loving God. Many of us can identify with their pain. Many of us have cried out to God: 'Lord, if you love me, why don't You deliver me from these difficult and distressing circumstances?'

The Israelites, confused, exhausted and bewildered by their ongoing suffering, especially the cruel edict that all Israelite boys were to be destroyed at birth, must have wondered, 'Where is God in all this? Has He forgotten His people's plight?' His seeming absence and inactivity raise the tension in the story, but we should not mistake these for indifference.

God was in fact working unobtrusively and steadily through human agents, even Egyptian ones in very high places (like Pharaoh's daughter) and especially through Moses. And at the right time, He acts: 'The Israelites groaned in their slavery and cried out, and their cry for help because of their slavery went up to God. God heard their groaning and remembered his covenant … So God looked on the Israelites and was concerned about them' (Exod. 2:23–25).

God *was* listening. We need to remind ourselves of this. He most definitely hears the groans of those who cry out to Him. The cry of the Israelites was not just a cry of pain but also a cry against the injustice and inhumanity with which they were being treated.

Let this sustain you in the midst of your disappointments and shattered dreams: God does not desert those of us who are in despair, confused by what appears to be a God who has forgotten us. Timing is everything with God. He supplies grace for every eventuality and if we draw on that grace in our situation, it will be more than a match for anything we're going through.

Romans 8:28 reminds us that 'in *all* things God works for the good of those who love him' (emphasis added). Nothing can happen to us that cannot, in time, bless us and bring good to us. Anything that happens to one of God's children has to pass through God's hands first, as we see from the opening chapters of Job.

However, this promise in Romans 8 does not necessarily mean that we shall always have problem-free lives, or that we will be protected from the selfish actions of others. For God to 'work for the good' is about God working in accordance with His own nature and goodness to conform us into the image of His Son. Rather than focusing on our journey, let's aim to focus primarily on God's love for us, and our love for Him.

Freedom in Christ means we have the power, if we so choose, to submit to God's purposes for our lives, even if that means going through the disappointment of pain and loss. Here is Kay Warren's testimony to that truth, which she posted on her Facebook page. Kay is married to Rick Warren, an American church leader, pastor and author.

On July 18, 1985, I gave birth to our beloved gift of God, Matthew David Warren. Holding him in my arms that morning, I had no idea how dark the journey would get for him – and for those who love him. All I knew that bright morning was that I was madly in love with him, and could see nothing ahead but a mother's dreams of a good life for her son.

37

My pregnancy had been extremely difficult and included three months of TOTAL bed rest (not even able to get up to use the bathroom) due to a severe allergic reaction that temporarily crippled me and caused tremendous physical pain and discomfort. The doctors reassured me that I and the baby would be fine - but how could I be sure? What if the baby wasn't alright? What if I wasn't alright?

I remember Easter 1985 - I was sick in bed, unable to go to church. Rick took the kids to church and I stayed by myself for a few hours - the TV remote by my side as my only companion. Somehow I dropped the remote and couldn't retrieve it, so there I was, alone on one of the most joyous holidays, with not even a TV preacher to keep me company, full of anxiety and fear for myself and my unborn child.

I painfully reached for my Bible and it fell open to Habakkuk 3:17-19 (NIV): 'Though the fig tree does not bud and there are no grapes on the vines, though the olive crop fails, and the fields produce no food, though there are no sheep in the pen and no cattle in the stalls, yet I will rejoice in the LORD, I will be joyful in God my Savior. The Sovereign LORD is my strength; he makes my feet like the feet of a deer, he enables me to go on the heights.'

This was a word from the Lord to me and I determined that even IF my worst nightmares came true - if my baby died, or I never walked again - that I would trust in God my Savior; I would rejoice in the Sovereign Lord.

Matthew David Warren was born and everything seemed fine. But by his first birthday, we began to wonder. And by his second and third birthdays, we knew he wasn't like his older sister and brother. As time unfolded, so did his struggles and I couldn't help but feel that my challenging pregnancy had negatively affected his developing brain and nervous system.

When he took his life last year – after battling and fighting so hard for decades – a friend sent me Habakkuk 3:17-19 in a sympathy card. She had no idea this passage was incredibly significant to me, but it was a fitting 'bookend' to his life. Because I had feared for years that he would take his life – it became his greatest pursuit and my deepest anguish – I had to come to the point in which I said as I had 27 years before: 'EVEN IF my worst nightmare comes true and he takes his life, I WILL rejoice in the Lord; I will be joyful in God my Savior.'

So today, his 29th birthday, through weeping I shout it to the watching universe: I will rejoice in the Lord; I will be joyful in God my Savior. My heart remains wounded and battered, but my faith is steady. There is, and will be, as Steven Curtis Chapman says, a 'glorious unfolding' of all that God has in store for me and my family. God is faithful to his promises of rebuilding and restoring the ruins and I am confident that I will yet be a witness to many, many, many lives healed and hope restored, all because of my beloved gift of God, Matthew David Warren. I miss you, darling boy ... but it will just be for a little while.

A Jewish Rabbi, Harold Kushner, watched his son die of a terrible disease that speeds up the ageing process. When his son, Aaron, died in his teens, he looked more like an old man of ninety. Kushner wrestled with this and wrote a bestselling book entitled, *When Bad Things Happen to Good People* (Pan, 2002). His thesis was that something had happened in the universe and that God's power to prevent distress and suffering was therefore limited.

The book stayed in the bestseller lists for months, obviously touching a chord with many people struggling with lost hopes and shattered dreams. It made sense to them because it offered some kind of explanation for suffering. People want to make sense of what God is (or apparently is not) doing. Why? Because we find it too uncomfortable to live with confusion and mystery.

Harold Kushner's book does not offer a traditional Christian view of suffering and perhaps we need here to remind ourselves of what the Bible teaches us about suffering.

God is all-powerful and all-loving

Is everything that happens in the world what God ideally wants, ie is everything 'God's will'? Christians believe that God is omnipotent (all-powerful): He can do anything He chooses that is consistent with His character (2 Tim. 2:13). God created human beings with the capacity to love, create, choose, make moral judgments, think, feel and worship. We were created to be in a relationship with Him, a relationship of love, not fear. Sadly, however, we find in Genesis chapters 2 and 3 the account of how Adam and Eve, the first human beings, used their power of choice – their free will – to turn away from God's love. They abused their free will, were disobedient and hid when they heard God's voice. Sin entered our world. Since then, the whole moral universe has been thrown into chaos and disorder. The presence of tragedy, pain and suffering in our world does not contradict

God's power or love; rather it is the consequence of the choices we made when we were given our freedom.

Yet, although human free will affects the details of our life on earth, God is Sovereign (see, for instance, 1 Chron. 29:11–12; Dan. 4:34–35 and Psa. 29:10). Our God is ultimately in control of everything. His actions and purposes are never absolutely dependent on human actions. His purposes are being worked out in spite of our free will.

It is important to remember that we are living in an 'in between' time, between the reality of what things are and what God promises they will be – '"He will wipe every tear from their eyes. There will be no more death" or mourning or crying or pain, for the old order of things has passed away' (Rev. 21:4).

The Bible also teaches us that God is completely loving and compassionate towards us. He shares our grief. Isn't that an amazing thought? Isaiah 63:9 tells us that God grieved with Israel: 'In all their distress he too was distressed'. God's heart was full of grief when He saw how His people were behaving before the flood: 'The LORD saw how great the wickedness of the human race had become on the earth, and that every inclination of the thoughts of the human heart was only evil all the time. The LORD regretted that he had made human beings on the earth, and his heart was deeply troubled' (Gen. 6:5–6).

The greatest example of God's compassion for us is Jesus. And He is God's response to human suffering.

GOD'S RESPONSE

Someone has said:

> Suffering is not a question that demands an answer;
> It is not a problem that demands a solution;
> It is a mystery which demands a presence.

Commenting on this profound statement in the final address at the Keswick Convention in 2008, Dr John Wyatt, Professor of Neonatal Paediatrics at University College London, said, 'And that's exactly what God does. He doesn't explain the mystery of evil and suffering, He enters into it. The Incarnation is the greatest example of empathy the cosmos has ever seen. That is Christ's way, Christ's example to us.'[1]

Jesus took our humanity, came to this world spoilt by sin and death and lived as one of us, in a human family, with all its joys and sorrows. Jesus knows what it's like to be disappointed, to lose a loved one, to be misunderstood and misjudged by those closest to Him – and He knows what it's like to stare death in the face and know that there's no escape. But on the cross He dealt not only with our sinfulness but also with our woundedness. In His body He carried 'our sorrows' (Isa. 53:4, NLT).

So today, we can take all our pain and disappointment to Jesus. We can tell God how we feel. If you are angry – tell Him. If you're full of despair – tell Him. There's no need to hold back your emotions – God knows anyway. And if you weep, God weeps with you.

Jesus at the cross also showed us the most defiant answer of faith we can use against present suffering – worship. Jesus' cry from the cross, 'My God, my God, why have you forsaken me?' (Matt. 27:46) was echoing the opening words of Psalm 22, which continues, 'My

God, I cry out by day, but you do not answer, by night, but I find no rest. Yet you are enthroned as the Holy One' (Psa. 22:1–3). We worship God for who He is, for His character – His love, His mercy, His power, His compassion, His faithfulness, His steadfastness, His deliverance. And as God is unchanging (unlike our circumstances) we can praise Him IN everything (not FOR everything).

Worship in times of trial, suffering, darkness and despair tells Satan that we *know* we are in God's hands, not his – we mustn't be blind to this truth. We are in the hands of an all-loving and all-powerful Father.

Changing the question

There is nothing intrinsically wrong with asking 'Why?' – pursuing possible answers and searching for reasons – but if at the end of the process we can't come to any useful conclusions, it's time to let go.

Rick Warren said after the death of his son: 'Explanations don't comfort. You won't feel better if you know why. It won't hurt any less.'

In the first chapter of his Gospel, Luke describes Gabriel's announcement to Mary that she, a young unmarried girl, is to bear the Son of God. Mary doesn't ask, 'Why?' or 'Why me?' Instead her response is 'How?' (Luke 1:34). If we go on asking, 'Why me?' about the loss of our hopes and dreams, we get nowhere. It may sometimes help to put things in perspective if we ask instead, 'Why *not* me?' However, if, instead of asking *why* we ask ourselves how we can handle the situation, the disappointment, in a way that brings glory to God, then we shall find a greater measure of peace. This is the place of submission. If we pray, 'Here I am, Lord. I'm not going anywhere without You; help me to grow closer to You in this painful place', He takes us in His arms, soothes our souls, binds our wounds and fills our minds with wisdom for the path ahead.

REFLECTION

'Friends, when life gets really difficult, don't jump to the conclusion that God isn't on the job. Instead, be glad that you are in the very thick of what Christ experienced. This is a spiritual refining process, with glory just around the corner … So if you find life difficult because you're doing what God said, take it in [your] stride. Trust him. He knows what he's doing, and he'll keep on doing it' (1 Pet. 4:12–13,19, *The Message*).

ACTIVITY

If we ask God, 'Why?' and there seems to be no answer, what is our response?
- That we don't trust Him?
- That we don't believe He's in control?
- That He is not the giver of good gifts?
- That He doesn't have our best interests at heart?
- Something else?

Think about your answers to these questions and ask God if there is anything He wants to reveal to you about your situation.

PRAYER

Lord, You know that the pain of the disappointment I'm feeling has brought me to the point of despair. Help me to trust You, and to begin my journey through this pain, not with the weight of my loss but with the certainty that You are a loving Father and that You want to use this to bring me closer to Yourself. Amen.

[1]www.christiantoday.com/article/costly.empathy.is.the.way.of.christ.keswick.convention.hears

CHAPTER FOUR

THE BUMPY TRACK

Grief is a normal reaction to disappointment and shattered dreams, and it invariably takes us on a journey that feels really bumpy, emotionally and mentally. Whilst a life without any expectations or goals would not be a healthy one, the degree to which we experience these 'bumps' on the track will depend to some extent on how insistent we are about holding onto our dreams and how much we cling to the belief that our expectations *ought* to be realised. One characteristic of this stage of the journey through disappointment is that we may frequently find that our hopes are raised in small ways, only to be dashed again so that we feel disappointed once more. It's important to recognise these minor 'dips' and determine, by God's grace, to press on despite the bumpiness of the track.

As Christians it is our responsibility on this bumpy track to bring our desires and expectations into line with God's desires and expectations for us. Paul expressed something of this desire for himself in his letter to the Christians in Philippi:

No, dear brothers, I am still not all I should be, but I am bringing all my energies to bear on this one thing: Forgetting the past and looking forward to what lies ahead, I strain to reach the end of the race and receive the prize for which God is calling us up to heaven because of what Christ Jesus did for us. (Phil. 3:13–14, TLB)

THE FIVE AREAS AFFECTED BY UNMET EXPECTATIONS AND DESIRES

God has created us to be whole people (spirit, soul and body – see 1 Thess. 5:23). It is widely thought that 'the soul' refers to our thoughts, feelings and decisions – in other words, our minds, emotions and wills. When our desires and expectations are not met, the loss will affect, in some way or other, every part of us: our emotions, our thinking and our behaviour, which in turn affect the way we feel physically. In addition, of course, our dashed hopes will stretch and challenge our faith.

The following diagram shows our five areas of functioning:

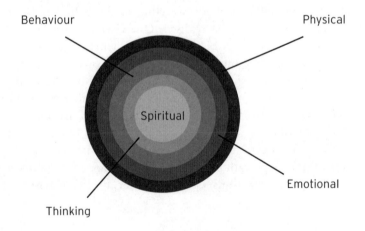

46

The 'Spiritual' is the inner core, where our deepest longings and thirsts are located – the desire for security, self-worth and significance. The next circle, 'Thinking', is everything involved in our rational, thinking selves, such as specific thoughts, beliefs, values and plans. The circle labelled 'Behaviour' is sometimes known as volitional; it makes the connection between what we are thinking and the end goals we hope to achieve. It is here that we make choices about how to behave. The 'Emotional' area covers our feelings and these often signal where our difficulties lie. The final circle is the 'Physical', which relates to the physical state of our bodies.

The five areas are interrelated and so can affect each other. Think about an apple for a moment: sometimes you cut one open only to find that it's beginning to go bad in the middle. Inevitably, if you left that apple for a bit longer, it would go bad all the way through. This is an illustration of what can happen to the different areas of our lives. If you're not handling your emotions well, that can affect the way you think – which can then have a knock-on effect on your behaviour. As we are spiritual, whole beings, when we are involved in any sort of inner conflict, all five areas of functioning are usually affected. We may sense a physical change – tension in the stomach or hot clammy hands; then our emotions become aroused with uncomfortable feelings. Our thoughts will also begin to change and may become distorted.

So, when we are reeling from the impact of disappointment on our lives, any or all of these five areas of functioning can be affected. On a *physical* level we may suffer from sleeplessness, loss of appetite, nausea, loss of libido, migraine or various other aches and pains. Our *behaviour* may change so that

47

we either withdraw from social contact altogether or become frenetically busy, trying to fill the 'hole' inside us. We may find ourselves *thinking* strangely, especially blaming ourselves or thinking we're inadequate or useless or generally no good, or we may be dogged by negative thoughts that in turn affect our *emotions*. All these areas affect us **spiritually** as well and we shall consider that in more detail in Chapter 5, Struggle Lane.

THE BUMPS ON THE TRACK

Our thoughts and emotions can be all over the place as we adjust to the loss of our hopes and dreams. The way in which we process our thoughts and feelings along the bumpy track is important. It's not about suffering stoically or even enjoying or wanting the experience. If we avoid or ignore our feelings or run away from them, we'll get stuck on the journey. It is therefore essential to stop investing energy into pushing these emotions away; instead we need to embrace them, giving them permission to be there. We identify below several thought patterns and emotions that can frequently be part of a grieving reaction, but this is not an exhaustive list! We can experience: negative and distorted thought patterns, anxiety, anger, guilt, a sense of inadequacy, regret, sadness, despair, unforgiveness, self-pity and jealousy. These are the 'bumps on the track' that we can't go around or under! All we can do is hold tight, face them, ride them and renounce them. Let's look at them one at a time.

Negative thought patterns

When we have suffered disappointment, it's easy to fall into a negative way of thinking and if we're not careful we find that these negative thought patterns become a habit. We may find ourselves constantly thinking, 'If only such and such hadn't happened', or 'If only I'd done this instead of that'. Or we think, 'What if …' – a thinking pattern which is dealt with more fully in 'Anxiety' below. We may find ourselves feeling regret for a particular course of action that we believe has contributed to the disappointment and we can't get out of that 'cycle' and move forward. What recurring negative thoughts come into your mind when you think about your disappointment?

It's really important to understand that negative thought patterns *can* be changed. You don't have to keep thinking negatively. Here are some effective methods in working through this bump on the track:

Challenge your thoughts – what *evidence* is there for what you keep thinking? For example, if you find yourself thinking, 'God must be punishing me', ask yourself, 'What does the Bible say about that?' Remind yourself that Jesus took the punishment for all our sins and foolishness when He died on the cross – Jesus has borne it. God doesn't punish His children. So there is no evidence for the thought 'God must be punishing me'. If you find yourself thinking, 'I'm a terrible person', remind yourself of all the verses in Scripture where God declares His love for us as individuals, eg Jeremiah 31:3, 'I have loved you with an everlasting love'.

Replace the negative thought with a new, healthy thought: 'I am a child of God. God loves me. He will not allow anything into my life unless there is a purpose to it. His grace is sufficient for my needs today/right now.' There are always two ways of looking at a situation. When the young shepherd boy, David, with his sling and pebbles, was confronted by Goliath, a giant in full armour, he could have thought negatively: 'He's huge – I'm off!' Or he could have thought positively: 'He's huge – I can't miss!' We know which David chose – and we know what happened as a result. Choose to look positively at situations.

Take the negative thought 'captive' and make it obedient to Christ. In this way we can 'conquer' thoughts with Scriptural truths; these truths are what God says about us. In his second letter to the Christians in Corinth, the apostle Paul writes this:

> For though we live in the world, we do not wage war as the world does. The weapons we fight with are not the weapons of the world. On the contrary, they have divine power to demolish strongholds. We demolish arguments and every pretension that sets itself up against the knowledge of God, and we take captive every thought to make it obedient to Christ.
>
> (2 Cor. 10:3–5)

Anxiety

Anxiety arises from an expectation that *results in an uncertain goal*. Chris Orme says:

> When I first lost my hearing, I didn't dare go into town alone for a whole year. My confidence had completely evaporated and I kept thinking, 'What if I can't understand what someone says to me?' From being something straightforward and so easily manageable that I did it without a second thought, getting on a bus to go shopping suddenly seemed impossible and generated a huge amount of anxiety – because of the uncertainty of achieving what until that point had been a very simple and

straightforward goal. This and other 'what if's, in a similar vein, meant I was very anxious indeed.

Uncertainty gives rise to the anxiety. How do we get over this bump on the track? How do we manage our anxiety?

Distraction is a simple but very effective way to cope with the anxiety and feelings of insecurity that can arise as we adjust to a new situation, ie the 'landscape' that has changed because of our shattered dream. Relating to the five areas of functioning, here are some practical ways to use distraction in the emotional, physical, thinking and spiritual areas of functioning:

- **Physical:** Focusing on the outside world can work to distract you, perhaps try going for a walk, listening to a conversation, looking at the colours people are wearing, or listing all the things you can hear, see, or touch. Relaxation can also help in countering anxiety. Here is a simple exercise for tuning into your body:

  Step 1: Stop what you are doing when you become anxious and emotionally raw.

  Step 2: Ground yourself by giving attention to the here and now. Notice any sounds you can hear. Become consciously aware of the experience of sitting in the chair (or standing). Feel the sensations in different parts of your body; focus your attention on the sensations of touch in your body where it is in contact with the chair or floor.

  Step 3: Focus on your breathing – the in-breaths and the out-breaths. Sooner or later your mind will wander off to find thoughts, images and to distract you with feelings – this is what the mind does! Bring your attention back to your breathing. This provides a way of disengaging from powerful thoughts and emotions and brings you back into the present. If you are very anxious and tense, then try to make your out-breath longer than your in-breath as this will relax you more.

- **Thinking:** Some people find mental exercise a distraction, for example engaging the mind in activities such as mental arithmetic, reciting poetry or scripture, doing crosswords or simply counting backwards from 100 by threes, eg 97, 94, 91 and so on. Mental exercise is a particularly useful technique during the night, when focusing on the outside world and on other people, as suggested above, may not be practical!

The 'traffic lights' distraction technique can be useful for stopping unhelpful thought processes. As soon as you start making negative statements about yourself, 'Oh, I'm no good; I'm a failure. This is terrible,' and so on, mentally picture a red traffic light, 'Stop! Red traffic light!' and say to yourself, 'I'm not going down that road.' At this point think of new, helpful thoughts and visualise the traffic light turning green, allowing you to move off down the road of your new thoughts.

Imagery techniques can also help alleviate anxiety. Imagine comforting homely images like being wrapped in a warm blanket. The use of imagery techniques can also be a very powerful aid to focusing on Christ. For instance, when an image associated with the anxiety comes into your mind, learn to replace it with an image of God as a strong tower or as the Rock on which you stand.

You can also distract yourself from anxious thoughts by the use of a bridging object. This is an object that represents security to you, perhaps associated with happy memories, eg a favourite teddy or a family photograph, and it works by helping to build a bridge from the anxiety-provoking 'here and now' to something that felt safe in the past or a specific memory that evokes good feelings.

- **Spiritual:** We can engage in the biblical approach to distraction by fixing our gaze upon God: 'And now, dear brothers and sisters, one final thing. Fix your thoughts on what is true, and honorable, and right, and pure, and lovely, and admirable. Think about things that are excellent and worthy of praise' (Phil. 4:8, NLT). Chris Ledger says:

When my daughter was first ill, I found it very hard to adjust to the reality of my shattered dream as I watched my previously active daughter become bedbound. In the middle of the night, anxious thoughts plagued me: 'What if this happens?' 'What if that happens?' Sleep became a rare commodity and I felt worn out. To manage the anxiety I learned to take a favourite worship song – *All hail the Lamb who reigns on high* – and sing it inwardly whenever my thoughts were running rampant in the middle of the night. Sometimes I would have to do this a number of times before the anxiety subsided, but over time the whole thing got easier as I replaced worrying with worshipping. After about a year, however, although the situation hadn't changed and my daughter was still ill, my anxiety levels had dramatically decreased as I found myself waking in the middle of the night with the words of the song already on my mind. I was slowly adjusting to my new story – one in which I had an ill daughter.

Isaiah 26:3 is also a wonderful promise: 'You will keep in perfect peace those whose minds are steadfast, because they trust in you.' This became a key verse for Chris Orme:

When I was a young teacher in a boarding school far from my home, I received a telephone message late one night to say that my father had collapsed with a brain haemorrhage and was in intensive care in a hospital in Oxford. After staying up most of the night to set work for my classes, I was driven to the station to catch the early train to London by the school's German teacher, a German national, who had been a student in the UK when World War II broke out and interned as an enemy alien. Her parents had perished in Auschwitz.

As I was boarding the train, the German teacher gave me a card with Isaiah 26:3 printed on it in German. On the back she had written an English paraphrase of the verse which read: 'You will keep in perfect peace *the one whose imagination stops at God.*' She explained to me at a later date how that particular verse was probably the main thing that had stopped her from going insane with grief when she discovered her family's fate. Our anxiety increases when our imaginations run riot, but if we can focus on God and His promises, letting our imaginations stop at God, the anxiety can be kept at bay.

Anger

Anger is not only a normal, healthy emotion (when we are able to identify and deal with the fear or hurt behind it) but a helpful emotion that responds to wrongdoing so that we can make things right. However, if we cannot control our anger, and it instead overcomes us, it can become extremely destructive both in our relationships and in our own quality of life. The Bible doesn't tell us that anger is a sin but that it can lead to sin: 'In your anger do not sin' (Eph. 4:26). The key is in how we process this emotion and express it.

Anger can include frustration, irritation and bitterness, all of which arise from an expectation *that has a blocked goal*. When we are faced with not getting what we have set our heart on (our goal) we will feel a measure of anger because, in this sense, we feel we have been robbed. So how do we get over this bump in the road? How can we manage our anger? Acknowledging and working through it is the healthy way forward.

- Step 1: Identify the root cause. Try writing down exactly what you are angry about. To see it plainly in black and white can sometimes reveal how trivial and forgivable the cause is. Or if it is quite rightly anger evoking, it will help you with the next step.
- Step 2: Tell God. Anger needs to be released otherwise if suppressed it can bubble inside us, causing havoc in our emotional area of functioning (and in turn affecting our other areas of functioning). God, unlike people, can take all the anger we can muster – all the rage and hurt. He is the safest person to release it to, and He knows all about it anyway. If you find this hard to do because you feel that anger is inherently wrong, remember Jesus showed His anger (Mark 11:15–17) and He has never sinned (2 Cor. 5:21).
- Step 3: Surrender the goal. We may very well be angry at a blocked goal that God doesn't actually want us to reach – or reach just yet. So we can 'give back' to God the lost hope, the shattered dream, the blocked goal, in return for His peace

and guidance. For example we could say: 'Lord, You know that I really wanted [dream/desire] but it has not happened. Maybe Your answer is "no" or "not yet", but I choose to hand it over, accept that You are in control and be comforted by the promise: "seek first his kingdom and his righteousness, and all these things will be given to you as well" (Matt. 6:33). You know my heart's desires, Lord. Thank You for what You've already done in my life and for what You're going to do.' Some people find it helpful to visualise handing the dream/ desire over to Jesus; putting it into His hands or laying it at the foot of the cross, then walking away. Chris Ledger used to visualise carrying her daughter to Jesus, who was sitting on a heavenly throne, and putting her daughter in His arms, then turning and walking away – so surrendering her daughter's future into Jesus' hands.

Guilt

This bump on the track arises from an expectation *that has an unrealistic and unreachable goal.* However hard we try we may never reach certain dreams or fulfil certain desires.

- It comes from thinking we are not good enough, not perfect enough, and can't please others enough, eg 'I should have been there for her'.
- It comes from breaking our own moral code, eg 'I must help my ill neighbour, but don't have the time'.
- It involves a fear of punishment.
- It's associated with shame and often wants to hide and/or cover up – see the story of Adam and Eve in Genesis 2–3.

How do we surmount the guilt-shaped bumps on the track? How do we manage feelings of guilt?

First we need to identify and understand the difference between conviction and condemnation. 'Godly sorrow [conviction] brings repentance that leads to salvation and leaves no regret, but worldly sorrow [condemnation] brings death' (2 Cor. 7:10). The Holy Spirit points out necessary change in us that is attainable (with His help). The devil points out change that is neither true nor possible for us. Once we understand this we can:

- Accept that our best is good enough – be realistic!
- Accept that life cannot be perfect and that we cannot be perfect.
- Accept forgiveness – from God and from other people where appropriate.
- Forgive ourselves where appropriate: we are all fallible, fallen human beings.

We often read that guilt is a useless emotion – is that true from a Christian perspective? The answer is yes and no! Guilt was designed by God to be a restraining and redeeming influence on fallen humanity. True guilt (conviction), when we acknowledge to ourselves that we have done something wrong, gives rise to repentance, accepting God's forgiveness and then putting whatever it is behind us and moving on. False or irrational guilt (condemnation) arises from something we can do nothing about and quite often involves something we failed to do. As 'there is no condemnation for those who are in Christ Jesus' (Rom. 8:1) we need to dismiss this false guilt because it serves no purpose at all. It just cuts us up.

Inadequacy

A sense of inadequacy results from the notion that something is lacking in us. When we aspire to attain a goal that gives us a sense of worth, but fall short of achieving it, we can feel very inadequate indeed:

> Alan was desperate to get a promotion at work because his identity and his sense of self-worth were based wholly on his status at work, rather than on his significance to God. So when he wasn't given the job he expected and desired, his self-esteem plummeted. He was left feeling angry and guilty that he had let his family down because now he wasn't going to bring home any extra money. He felt totally inadequate and a failure. Sadly, his status had become his god.

For some of us, a feeling of inadequacy comes from comparing ourselves with others. On the other hand we are all inadequate because we have all sinned and so fall short of the glory of God (see Rom. 3:23). Paul says in Romans 7:19: 'For I do not do the good I want to do, but the evil I do not want to do – this I keep on doing.' How do we get over the bump on the track labelled 'inadequacy'? How do we manage a sense of inadequacy?

We need to recognise that a sense of inadequacy is justified. On our own we cannot make things happen. Dr Larry Crabb, author, counsellor and Christian psychologist speaks in his book, *Shattered Dreams*, of what he describes as a liberating discovery:

> I am inadequate. My sense of inadequacy is not the effect of deficient intellect or poor training, nor ... a symptom of emotional disorder. It is the painful admission that in and of myself I can help no one ...

Awareness of inadequacy is neither a curse to lift nor a disorder to cure. It is a gift to be received.[1]

Chris Ledger says:

> I have discovered my own inadequacies in caring for my ill daughter over many years, and have come to accept that although I may be inadequate in some areas, that doesn't make me an inadequate person. I am learning to allow my inadequacies to drive me into a deeper dependency on God.

This is true for us all: no one is perfect; no one copes with everything! Christians are all just flawed-but-redeemed human beings and being inadequate in certain parts of our lives doesn't make us inadequate people.

In order to overcome our feelings of inadequacy, it is important to come back to God and remind ourselves how precious we are to Him. We are the apple of His eye (Psa. 17:8); we are precious in His sight (Isa. 43:4); God rejoices over us with singing (Zeph. 3:17); He lavishes His grace upon us (Eph. 1:7,8). His love doesn't depend upon what we do, but upon who we are – precious children of our heavenly Father.

Sadness

Another emotional pain associated with disappointment is sadness and sorrow. In coming to terms with our shattered dreams or dashed hopes we will all feel a degree of sadness as we grieve for what is no more or never was. The significance of our loss will affect the depth of our sadness: if a very close relationship has ended or a loved one has died we may feel a greater degree of sadness than if a friend moves away from the area. So it's important to allow ourselves to feel sad (provided that this doesn't turn into self-pity) and to let the tears flow. Like anger, forcing sadness 'underground' is neither helpful nor healthy. Here are some ways in which we can deal with sadness:

- Acknowledge the emotion and the cause of it. Perhaps write it down or talk to someone. To see or hear the words we say can help in coming to terms with what has happened and why we feel the way we do.
- Set a specific time during which sadness can be expressed. For some people, setting aside a specific time to feel sad about a disappointment can help. A time limit allows the important period of catharsis, yet prevents us from dwelling on our sorrow for too long. This can ultimately move us into a happier mood.
- Engage in an activity that expresses sadness. Creative activities such as dancing, painting, singing, playing an instrument etc can be helpful.
- Write a list of all the things you are thankful for and worship God for them. Remember He can make 'beauty' out of 'ashes', 'gladness' out of 'mourning' and a 'garment of praise' out of 'despair' (Isa. 61:3).
- Balance time between being social and being alone. Some find that being with people can drain them of energy, so it's important for them to have time alone to recharge and recover from sadness by excluding themselves from social settings, but it's important to ensure that this doesn't become a habit of withdrawal. Then there are those who find company comforting and energising. This should be balanced with time alone so that the individual can still acknowledge and work

through their sadness, rather than using others to constantly distract them from the pain.

If you are concerned that your degree of sadness, or that of the person you're helping, is worsening into depression, seek appropriate help (a GP or a counsellor). Depression can greatly affect the individual in all areas of functioning. Symptoms can include: difficulty sleeping, loss of appetite, lost interest in activities usually enjoyed, difficulty concentrating; feeling numb or irritable, amongst others. Visit www.nhs.uk or www.mind.org.uk for more information.

Despair

Be aware that sadness can turn into despair. Despair can arise when our hopes and dreams are dashed. As we come to terms with our disappointment it's not wrong to feel inadequate or to feel sorrow, but it's important not to let these feelings lead us to despair. We can experience a painful mix of hopelessness, distress, anguish and unhappiness, which may cause us to give up hope, lose heart, be despondent, become disconsolate, resigned and trapped under a cloud of melancholia. Then, despairing, we are tempted to throw in the towel and quit, instead of allowing these uncomfortable feelings to lead us into a deeper dependency on God our Father. 'Despair's arguments seemed so plausible in the dark, murky atmosphere of the harsh environment.'[2]

Turn to Jeremiah 20, and see what happened when the prophet Jeremiah was beaten and put in the stocks because he had spoken out God's truth. As a result of this beating and humiliation Jeremiah plunges into the depths of despair. In verses 7 to 12 he accuses God of deceiving him and screams out his hurt to the Almighty. But suddenly, in verse 13, the mood changes completely: 'Sing to the LORD! Give praise to the LORD! He rescues the life of the needy from the hands of the wicked'. Jeremiah has allowed God's truth to penetrate his innermost being to such an extent that in the very moment of being stretched and tested, he finds within himself a voice that shouts louder than his pain, a voice that gives praise to God. (You may recall that Paul and Silas had a similar experience in Philippi – see Acts 16:16–34.) However, Jeremiah's words of praise do not last long! He descends again into despair, questioning, in verse 14, why he was ever born. 'Faith and doubt are locked together within him and he finds it difficult to endure the strain of that tension.'³ The most important lesson to learn when struggling with discouragement and despair is that it is OK to be honest with God, telling Him exactly how we feel!

Chris Ledger's daughter, Julia, wrote:

I am mum to two delightful children, a son aged ten and a daughter aged eight, and I have been unwell with ME/Chronic Fatigue Syndrome for the past twenty-three years. For the last five years I have been severely affected and mostly in bed 24/7. I have felt the agony of not being able to be involved in my children's lives or see them taking part in school functions and performances. There has been one disappointment after another. Sadly, I will never regain these lost years with my children. I realise that, as a result, when I feel angry, powerless and helplessly frustrated, I can easily push the 'self-sabotage' button. For me this is a way to protect myself from the further pain of disappointment. Rather than hope and be disappointed yet again, I retreat to a place of despair that engulfs me like a black cloud. Disappointment ... I know all about it because that has been my experience for over half my life! But the only answer is to keep hanging on to God.

Regret

Regrets are a waste of time that spoil the present moment: 'those who let distress drive them away from God are full of regrets, end up on a deathbed of regrets' (2 Cor. 7:10, *The Message*). Yet there is no such thing as a life without regrets. Do you regret something you or someone else did or didn't do? Is the regret linked to a loss of expectation or that you feel disappointed that your goal hasn't been reached? When we first feel regret about something, it may be helpful to take stock, see where we made a mistake or a choice we're unhappy about in hindsight, learn from that experience, and then ask God's forgiveness – but after that we need to move on. If we don't do this and the regrets are allowed to play over and over in our heads we are just torturing ourselves with hurtful thoughts. Ask for God's help to leave those regrets in the past.

If we allow the 'record' of our regrets to play on a continuous loop in our heads, they can become so mentally painful that they turn into burdens that interfere with our present happiness, restrict our future and can cause 'road blocks'. When we feel regret we often re-live guilt, sadness or anger over and over again. Guilt and shame echo: 'How could you have done such a thing?' When tormented by feelings of guilt and self-hate we face a road block that impedes our moving on in the journey with God.

So it's important to identify and process these feelings in a healthy way. This includes admitting to ourselves the reason why the thing we regret happened in the first place, letting go of what we couldn't have controlled or changed, and taking responsibility for what could be done differently were we to face that situation again. This is not about putting ourselves down but about letting go of negative thoughts and feelings. Sometimes it's healthy and appropriate to grieve over the situation we regret. Allowing ourselves to experience these feelings fully, with the intention of moving forward, can help us to stop revisiting them.

In Luke 9:57–62, Luke briefly outlines several stories of men who were called by Jesus to follow Him; the response of the third was, 'I will follow you, Lord; but first let me go back and say goodbye to my family.' Jesus responded, 'No one who puts a hand to the plough and looks back is fit for service in the kingdom of God.' The sentiment may seem a little harsh, but it points to the truth that we are ineffective in our service and in our lives as Christians if we are constantly looking back, with regret as much as with anything else. The only positive reason for looking back is to see where we've come from and give thanks to God for all His goodness to us and for the progress that we've made by His grace. Regretful backward-looking serves no useful or helpful purpose whatsoever.

Unforgiveness
When we are battling disappointment and lost dreams, it's natural to want to blame somebody. We may feel very resentful and unable to forgive that person. As with anger, there is a perverse sense of strength in holding onto unforgiveness, but ultimately the only

person we hurt is ourselves. We do ourselves so much harm by having an unforgiving attitude. When others have hurt us, it's very important to forgive them; if we don't forgive, the seething anger and resentment can cause another road block, whereas forgiveness and compassion towards others will help us on the journey. Are you struggling with unforgiveness towards a certain person? Ask God to help you forgive and remind yourself that even if others fail you, God won't. 'Even if my father and mother abandon me, the LORD will hold me close' (Psa. 27:10, NLT).

Sometimes, of course, the person we blame and the one we find it hardest to forgive is ourselves. It is important to forgive ourselves for the words and actions we regret and to be as kind and compassionate to ourselves as we are to other people.

Looking back over his life, it's possible that Paul was disappointed with his early behaviour. It was at his feet that those who stoned Stephen laid their cloaks; it was the young Saul who channelled all his religious zeal into persecuting the members of the Early Church – 'Saul began to destroy the church. Going from house to house, he dragged off both men and women and put them in prison' (Acts 8:3). Yet, after his dramatic conversion experience (Acts 9) he was not held back by what he had done; he was able to forgive himself and move on – 'forgetting what is behind and straining towards what is ahead, I press on towards the goal to win the prize for which God has called me heavenwards in Christ Jesus' (Phil. 3:13–14)!

Self-pity

It's so easy to succumb to self-pity when we're struggling with disappointment, especially if we make the mistake of looking at other people who appear to have things so much easier than we do.

Self-pity ('poor old me!') may give us a twisted kind of pleasure for a short time but it can be very destructive. This kind of self-indulgence becomes not just another bump on the track but an actual road block; it's like stopping en route to hold a 'pity party'. We see ourselves as blameless victims who deserve sympathy and special consideration from everyone! It's not wrong to feel sorry for ourselves but 'wallowing in self-pity' (as Chris Orme's father used to put it), or being enticed into a 'pity party' where others encourage us to be as self-centred as they are, doesn't get us anywhere at all.

What we do with this feeling of self-pity is key to moving forward. Linda Harry says, 'There is only one way to end a self-pity cycle: stop comparing yourself to others, and simply follow Christ.'[4] As far as we can tell, Moses didn't waste time and energy feeling sorry for himself because he wasn't permitted to enter the promised land; instead he put all his energy into training up Joshua, his successor, and imparting to him fearless faith in the God who does not forsake His children. Life may not always make sense, but let's remind ourselves to trust Him even when things don't seem fair, and hold on to the wonderful knowledge that He is our Helper and Sustainer.

Jealousy
Jealousy often goes hand in hand with self-pity. It arises from a desire to have what other people have – what we feel we lack or have lost. We are in pain from the loss of our hopes and dreams and when we look around us we see other people still enjoying what we ourselves have lost.

Feeling jealous is an almost instinctive reaction and it's hard not to indulge in it. We constantly compare ourselves with others

– and that can be completely innocent. Where it gets dangerous is when we don't just compare but compete; we become driven by jealousy to be 'better than', 'cleverer than', 'richer than', 'slimmer than' and it can consume us. Unless we actually fall into the sin of damaging other people as a result of our jealousy, jealousy usually harms only ourselves, eating away at us, spoiling our joy in all the good things that remain despite our loss and disappointment.

These jealous feelings may start in an almost unnoticeable way – not so much red-hot jealousy as a fleeting sensation of envy – the thought, 'It's not fair' or a little flicker of resentment flitting through our minds. However, what is just a flicker today can turn into a fire tomorrow. Suppose you spotted a small flame in your house – not a fire as such and certainly not a huge blaze, but tiny tongues of heat dancing on the hem of a curtain or the side of the stove. What would you do? How would you react? Would you shrug your shoulders and walk away? Of course not! You would extinguish the fire. For the sake of your house you wouldn't entertain such fire.

For the sake of your heart the same is true. Heed the warnings in Scripture about the fires of our heart, which, if left unchecked can burst into hungry flames and consume all that can be consumed. King Solomon, renowned for his wisdom, said that jealousy is as 'unyielding as the grave. It burns like blazing fire, like a mighty flame' (Songs 8:6) and Paul was adamant that 'Love is patient and kind. Love is *not jealous*' (1 Cor. 13:4, NLT, emphasis added).

In John 21:21–22, it appears that Peter was jealous of John when he asked Jesus, 'Lord, what about him?' Jesus replied, 'what is that to you? You must follow me.' In other words, don't compare yourself (or your situation) with others. Accept God's ways for your life – keep your eyes fixed on Him. It's quite a challenge!

Perhaps we will be encouraged to follow it when we look at the possible consequences of jealousy:

- **Loneliness**: 'Anger is cruel and fury overwhelming, but who can stand before jealousy?' (Prov. 27:4). In a cemetery stands a headstone with the inscription, 'She died for want of things'. Alongside that headstone is another which reads, 'He died trying to give them to her'. What very sad epitaphs both are!

- **Sickness**: Solomon wrote, 'A heart at peace gives life to the body, but envy rots the bones' (Prov. 14:30). The person that jealousy damages most is the one who is jealous.

- **Hurting others**: For evidence of how jealousy can hurt others we have only to look at the familiar story of Joseph and his jealous older brothers. They started out by teasing him – normal sibling rivalry – but then, when his father made it very obvious that Joseph was the favourite son, 'His brothers were jealous of him' (Gen. 37:11). Soon it was easier to dump Joseph in a pit and lie to their brokenhearted father than to see Joseph at the dinner table. Before long, Joseph was in Egypt, the brothers were facing famine and their father was in the dark, his dreams for Joseph shattered, his hopes gone. He thought his son was dead – and all because of jealousy.

How do we get over this – often large – bump of jealousy? How do we manage this emotion, which can so easily take hold of us?

- **Trust God**: He is in control of what happens to you. 'Do not fret ... or be envious ... Trust in the LORD and do good' (Psa. 37:1,3). The root cause of jealousy is lack of trust in God: not believing that God will see to it that we have what we need. Jacob's sons, Joseph's brothers, didn't trust God to meet their needs and this led to destructive jealousy.

Three decades after a diving accident rendered Joni Eareckson Tada a quadriplegic, Joni and her husband, Ken, visited Jerusalem. Sitting in her wheelchair Joni remembered the story of Jesus healing the paralytic man at the pool of Bethesda. Thirty years earlier she'd read the account and asked Jesus to do the same for her.

That day in Jerusalem she thanked God that He had answered a higher prayer. Joni now sees her wheelchair as her prayer bench and her affliction as her blessing. Had God healed her legs thirty years previously, thousands of prayers for other people would have been sacrificed to her busy life. She sees that now. She accepts that now. Jealousy of the able-bodied people around her was eclipsed by gratitude as Joni surrendered her will to God's. Joni learned this important lesson: God withholds what we *desire* in order to give us what He sees that we *need*, eg, you desire a spouse, He gives you Himself; you desire a larger church, He gives you a strong church; you want to be healed so that you may serve, He wants you confined so that you can pray. Joni trusted her heavenly Father with her disability. She chose not to allow jealousy of able-bodied people to steal her joy.

Physical effects of disappointment

Having looked at how our emotions can give us a bumpy ride and sometimes cause road blocks, let's briefly stop and identify how these emotions may affect our physical body. We are made in God's image, with all five areas of human functioning mysteriously working together, so it makes sense that if our emotions are all over the place, our body will also be affected. This can include experiencing:

- Lethargy/insomnia
- Heart palpitations/butterflies in the stomach
- Nausea
- Stomach upsets/irritable bowel syndrome
- Trembling/shaking/tingling sensations
- Migraines
- Blurred vision
- Dizziness/faintness

These symptoms may occur when we are facing and trying to process a deep pain of disappointment and loss. Having practical and prayerful support, and someone to talk to, is essential. The relaxation exercise in this chapter (page 51 under 'Anxiety' section) can be beneficial. It may be appropriate to seek out professional help if these symptoms are frequent and greatly affect daily life.

REFLECTION
Thyra, whose only daughter, a 'miracle baby', died of cancer aged just thirty-nine, testifies to God's working in her life, and bringing her desires into line with His for her.

There were three of us at her bedside just a little while ago when my beautiful thirty-nine-year-old daughter died quietly of lung cancer. Besides her Dad and me, her very close special friend stood faithfully by her until the end. As she gently drew her last breath he found himself thinking, 'I have always had faith that she will be healed and now she has just died - this just can't be happening.' Such

70

poignant disappointment raises so many issues for us and for me too at this time as her deeply grieving mother.

The dictionary defines 'disappointment' as unfulfilled desire or expectation. I certainly desired as passionately as is humanly possible, along with her father and her friend and so many others, that she would be healed, and soon too. I also came to realise that, despite our prayers not being answered as we'd hoped, God has not failed us here and He Himself is the answer to those disappointments we have that involve Him.

God's ways are higher than our ways and so it stands to reason that there are many times when what He ordains disappoints us. This is because *we* need adjusting and not Him. It is our frailty that shapes our desires. By frailty I mean that place of imperfection at which we have arrived in our journey as God's beloved-but-still-growing children. In that place, your desires and mine are still so much under the influence of the world, the flesh and the devil. Our values are not yet perfect kingdom values though they may be looking pretty good. This means that we live and move and have our being from a less than trustworthy foundation. So our desires are bound to fall short of what the perfect child of God would desire.

I remember encouraging my daughter, who longed to be a wife and mum and to have a second shot at serving God with all her heart, to take her desires to God for Him to work on. In my heart was the belief that she was dying and that He would compassionately and lovingly bring her desires in line with that reality. Once He had done that, whatsoever she asked in His name would materialise.

I later saw her desires become simply to die well. And that she was gloriously enabled to do.

On my own journey with God, which began forty-nine years ago, He has taken my desires a very, very long way from what they used to be. How often I have sung *Change my heart, oh God* and how readily over all those years has He worked on me, with such a long, steady, patient outpouring of grace. That brought me a year ago, when Shirley's cancer was diagnosed, to that blessed place where I have not been angry with God for not doing as I wanted. Don't think I have been slow in asking for complete and immediate healing – my fists became raw from beating on His door – but always undergirding my passion was the radical caveat, *nevertheless, Thy will be done and not mine.* I did not like the way things seemed to be going but at least I was actually able to surrender to it. This is what all the years of His shaping my heart made possible. The shift in me was away from governance by my puny wanting, to submission to His glorious desires and sovereignty. This is why I could pray, when in the years before the cancer struck she was lost and floundering, *Do whatever it takes to bring my lovely child into your kingdom.* This is why at the time of her death I could accept the implications of that with a degree of peace and contentment. Perhaps I can say I was no longer truly disappointed by the outcome of all my pleading with God, although I am certainly still writhing under the huge pain of it.

At some stage I'm supposed to know joy, I believe, but I'm a very long way from that right now. What I have come to realise about pain is that it is the fertile soil God uses to nurture whatever character and whatever change of desires He needs in me for the future task He has in mind for me. Because I have a fallen nature, tough measures such as losing my only child can, because of their severity, serve towards me making progress. God can use the most awful circumstances of our lives in this way. The snag would be if I refused to seize what is actually an opportunity and to co-operate. In my case it is in my pain that God can work for good (Rom. 8:28). Such pain and many other circumstances are the mechanisms God uses to bring us in line with His sovereignty. My darling girl has run her race and completed the task set before her. I see her passing on the baton – the challenge is that I do not drop it but run my race well too, continuing where she left off.

ACTIVITY

As Thyra has so honestly and poignantly described, we are all fallible human beings who by nature want to live our lives independently of God. We are all naturally inclined to be self-dependent, rather than God-dependent. In the Old Testament God says: 'My people have committed two sins: They have forsaken me, the spring of living water, and have dug their own cisterns, broken cisterns that cannot hold water' (Jer. 2:13). Rather than looking to God and growing a relationship with Him in which we feel secure, worthwhile and significant, we tend to try and meet these deep spiritual needs elsewhere, only to find that we are searching in 'empty cisterns'.

Spend some time before God asking him to show you any areas of your life where you have 'dug your own cistern' –

73

looking for fulfilment or satisfaction outside of God's purposes for you. Confess them to Him and ask Him to fill you afresh with the 'living water' that can satisfy your soul.

PRAYER

Father, I confess to You that so often I have looked in the wrong places for real fulfilment. Give me a thirst for Your living water and teach me to drink deeply and to be satisfied in You. Amen.

[1] Dr L. Crabb, *Shattered Dreams* (New York: Waterbrook Press, 2001), p76

[2] H. Rolston, *Beyond the Edge* (Nottingham: Inter-Varsity Press, 2008) p92

[3] S. Hughes, *Every Day with Jesus*: July/August 2014 issue (Farnham: CWR, 2014)

[4] strangewondrous.net/browse/author/h/harry+linda

CHAPTER FIVE

STRUGGLE LANE

You've reached the end of the Bumpy Track; there may well still be a few bumps ahead here and there but the really bumpy stretch is done with. However, the journey isn't over yet and you may now find yourself in Struggle Lane. Struggling is what we do in order to come to terms with the disappointment. There are ways to help yourself, or those you're helping, on Struggle Lane, and they can be grouped under five headings.

1. RECOGNISE AND ACKNOWLEDGE YOUR STRUGGLE

How do we respond when life throws an unexpected trial into our path? Regretfully we may respond in the following ways:

- **Self-pity.** 'It's not fair!' – this little sentence is quite possibly the one that parents hear most often when their brood is growing up! It almost always arises from one sibling believing that another sibling has a better deal. Self-pity is tempting. It's easy to think that others have an easier load or more favourable circumstances. Maya Angelou once remarked, 'Self-pity in its early stages is as snug as a feather mattress. Only when it hardens does it become uncomfortable.'

- **A hardened determination to survive.** This can appear to work but it involves growing a tough skin and the danger is that we block out all feelings and are unable to sympathise with others in their need.
- **Relentless demands for others to see and care about our pain.** This can lead to very manipulative behaviour, which brings more problems than it solves.
- **A decision to hide and let no one see the pain.** We struggle alone. As Christians we're not meant to do that.
- **Ignoring the pain.** We deny the disappointment; we may play the clown, using humour as a shield, hoping that laughter will keep the anguish at bay.
- **Working hard.** This can take our minds off the disappointment – but only temporarily.
- **Relieving the pain in any way we can.** This can lead to various addictions: overeating, self-harm, anorexia, pornography, alcohol, drugs … These of course offer only temporary relief and bring a host of other problems in their wake.
- **Getting angry with everyone who crosses our path.** This solves nothing.
- **Doing whatever helps, like reading or spiritual retreats.** These are fine in themselves but unless we acknowledge the struggle and the pain and the disappointment, they are not going to resolve anything in the long term.
- **Distancing ourselves from God.** There's a very negative progression here:

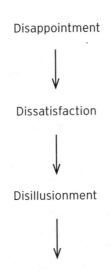

Disappointment

↓

Dissatisfaction

↓

Disillusionment

↓

Distancing ourselves from God

Some of us, because we have been disappointed in the past, have chosen simply not to want very much because it seems more straightforward that way. But that's stoicism, not Christianity. When we withhold our lives from God, those lives get smaller, more self-centred and increasingly distant from God. As this happens, we can get angry with God, blaming Him for the painful events of life, 'Why did You do this to me, God?'

Some of the options mentioned involve denying the pain and disappointment – the opposite of acknowledging – which will all be unsatisfactory in the long term.

We need to be honest about our pain and about the struggles that it brings. Shattered dreams can produce pain so excruciating that sometimes we wonder if we can survive.

Such pain is not evidence of a weak faith; it's evidence that we are normal! Something wonderful can survive something terrible. The resurrection came after the horror and pain of the cross. Feel your pain. Regard your brokenness as an opportunity that reveals an awareness that you long to be someone you're not, someone you can't be without divine help. Feel the soul-piercing pain of disappointment. If you are reading this book because you are in a position where you are trying to help someone struggling with this kind of disappointment, don't try to 'rescue' them too quickly from their struggle. The struggle is an important part of the process. As someone has said, the definition of a mature Christian is one who struggles well.

Struggling in this way is nothing new. It is evident from many of the Psalms that David struggled with disappointment and emotional pain and he expresses his struggle vividly and honestly. In Psalm 77:1–14, he cries out from his heart:

> I cried out to God for help;
> I cried out to God to hear me.
> When I was in distress, I sought the Lord;
> at night I stretched out untiring hands,
> and I would not be comforted.
> I remembered you, God, and I groaned;
> I meditated, and my spirit grew faint.
> You kept my eyes from closing;
> I was too troubled to speak.
> I thought about the former days,
> the years of long ago;
> I remembered my songs in the night.

My heart meditated and my spirit asked:
'Will the Lord reject for ever?
Will he never show his favour again?
Has his unfailing love vanished for ever?
Has his promise failed for all time?
Has God forgotten to be merciful?
Has he in anger withheld his compassion?'
Then I thought, 'To this I will appeal:
the years when the Most High stretched out his right hand.
I will remember the deeds of the LORD;
yes, I will remember your miracles of long ago.
I will consider all your works
and meditate on all your mighty deeds.'
Your ways, God, are holy.
What god is as great as our God?
You are the God who performs miracles;
you display your power among the peoples.

Although David was in deep distress, he was able to recall times when God had acted on his behalf, and on behalf of His people. David turns his eyes from his problems and disappointments to God's character and God's adequacy, which has never failed in the past and will not fail David now. David had grasped the truth that God was bigger than any situation he faced. Our problem can be that we look at God through our disappointments, instead of looking at our disappointments through God. If God, the Creator and Sustainer of the universe, loves us so much that He sent Jesus to die in our place, thus breaking the power of sin and death, surely He is able to help us in all our struggles with disappointment and heartbreak. David reflected on God's past goodness and that strengthened his trust for the present.

2. RECOGNISE THAT JESUS IS WITH YOU

In Chapter Three we stated that Jesus Himself knew disappointment. There are many instances in the New Testament of Jesus experiencing pain and disappointment. He was even rejected by those He passionately loved: 'He came to … his own, but his own did not receive him' (John 1:11). Jesus knows our pain more deeply than anyone else could, but more, He is where we find our hope again.

Think back to the story of the disciples on the Emmaus Road (Luke 24:13–35). Luke records that they stood still with 'downcast' faces – they were, in modern parlance, 'gutted'. They didn't perceive that God in Jesus was walking beside them. Were their spiritual eyes closed because they were so distracted by the emotional pain of their disappointment? Nearing the village where they lived, Jesus made as if to go on and they invited Him to stay with them. Jesus accepted the invitation (does He ever refuse?) and in the moment when He broke the bread the glorious truth of the resurrection dispelled their disappointment and they saw the Lord of hope. Reflecting on the experience they exclaimed, 'Were not our hearts burning within us while he talked with us on the road and opened the Scriptures to us?' (v32). Talking with Jesus and reading the Bible focuses our eyes upon Him rather than on the disappointment.

3. RECOGNISE WHETHER YOU ARE TRUSTING GOD AND WHAT YOU ARE TRUSTING GOD *FOR*

'Trust God,' is almost always good advice, although it can be said glibly, or thoughtlessly or as an automatic 'spiritual' response and therefore add to the pain that someone is already suffering.

The word 'trust' in Hebrew signifies 'to lean with the whole body, to rest the full weight upon'. This means we don't try to go it alone by endeavouring to hold ourselves up; instead 'trusting the Lord' requires us to lean our whole weight upon Him. It also means abandoning ourselves, our hopes and dreams into His hands.

The struggle to trust

What stops us from trusting God? Not knowing the end result? For most of us, it would be easier to trust if we knew we wouldn't have to face any more disappointments and hurts, and were certain of the outcome we desired!

Whether we believe that God causes our difficulties or that He merely allows trials into our lives, one thing is clear: He could have prevented the disappointment and the pain that we are undergoing. That creates a tension – a struggle. We can choose how we react – will we become rebellious? Will we become apathetic? Will we turn our backs on God? It's at this point in the struggle that we need to be rooted in our faith and not in our feelings. It is not about God exercising healing, protection or deliverance (although He does this from time to time), rather, it is about believing that God acts justly in *everything*. Not our idea of justice, but God's! 'Though he slay me, yet will I hope in him' (Job 13:15). Faith determines that no matter what may come, we remain unshakeable in our conviction that God loves us.

Faith begins and ends with trusting God's word.

Part of our struggle in trusting God is accepting the following:

- Life includes suffering, but God, in the place of our own suffering, is there with us.
- The way to handle suffering is to discover our desire for God – enter into our thirst; feel the ache; face our disappointment.
- Life offered to us in Jesus is a gift of grace and love.

What are you trusting God *for*?

In the early years of her daughter's illness, a friend asked Chris Ledger over coffee: 'What are you trusting God *for*?' Chris comments: 'On reflection, I realised that I was looking too much at the shattered dream and not totally at how I could find wholeness in Christ. I started to alter my focus, and although the situation didn't change, I began to cope better.'

What are we trusting God *for*? A husband/wife? A new job? A child? Healing from cancer for a family member? Or are we trusting Him that whatever happens, He has our best interests at heart and is on our side? 'If God is for us, who can be against us?' (Rom. 8:31). Are we trusting that nothing – but nothing – can separate us from the love of God? That He will give us strength day by day to face our pain?

Whilst we are in Struggle Lane we may find ourselves still wrestling with questions that we've encountered before: we may still feel angry with God or abandoned by Him, even rejected. We may still be asking, 'Why, God?', wondering why He allowed something to hurt us or why He won't allow us to have something that seems good to us. As we struggle with these thoughts and emotions it may be helpful to consider just what it is that we are trusting God for.

- Are we trusting God in order to have a good time? No!
- Are we trusting God for the pain to be deadened, to deny or ignore it (the way of Buddha)? No!
- Are we trusting for God to answer our prayers in the way we want? No – that's a dangerous one!
- Are we trusting God in order to deepen our desire for the Lord Jesus Christ, for His strength, comfort and grace? Yes!
- Are we trusting in God's character – a Father who is for us, who will never leave us, and loves us unconditionally? Yes!

4. RECOGNISE THE IMPORTANCE OF RELINQUISHMENT: SURRENDERING OUR HOPES AND DREAMS

Our fondest dreams for this life, the ones we naturally believe are essential to our happiness, must be fully abandoned if we are to grow closer to God through our experience of shattered dreams. Pain exposes our commitment to personal happiness for what it really is: an arrogance that displaces God from His rightful place. Pain has the potential for good. It can be a tool in God's hands; used to shape our characters and draw us closer to Him.

Acknowledging God's claim on our lives, even when submitting to that claim brings pain, we need to choose humility and submission to the will of God over our 'rights'. Here is Chris Ledger's testimony to how God challenged her on this issue at a time when she was exhausted from looking after her chronically ill daughter:

I had arranged a weekend break from caring by attending a conference. This was a time for me to get away from the situation and recharge my batteries. Going to bed on the

Saturday night I was reminded of Jesus' words, 'Whoever wants to be my disciple must deny themselves and take up their cross and follow me. For whoever wants to save their life will lose it, but whoever loses their life for me will find it' (Matt. 16:24-25). I thought I had handed ownership of Julia to Him, but now I was being challenged at a much deeper level. God was asking me to lay down all my rights. Having been brought up in a culture of consumer rights, patient rights, human rights, animal rights and civil rights - to name but a few - I realised that this belief in 'my rights' had permeated my thinking and to some extent I was still demanding from God my right to have a daughter who was able to live a normal life. How could I think like this? I was ashamed as I discovered the depths of my selfishness, 'demandingness' and self-centredness. I had no rights - I deserved nothing - all that I possessed was a free gift from God by His grace.

Responding to what God was showing me, I began to identify all the rights that I was consciously holding on to, by putting each one onto a sticky note. I wrote: I give up my rights to see Julia:

- well and growing into her full potential
- having fun, laughing and enjoying life
- being independent and driving a car
- being able to fly abroad and have a holiday
- enjoying walking in the sunshine
- married with children
- having a career in nursing.

This was painful but I knew I had to push on and face the dark areas of my self-centredness. Feeling convicted to the core of my being I moved on to write out all my selfish desires - each one on a separate note: I want to be:

- free from the responsibilities of caring so that I can do what I want with my time
- free from dealing with the emotional pain of sadness, anger, guilt, despair, helplessness and hopelessness
- free from the struggle to hang on to God and trust His promises
- free to spend more time with John and to be able to go away together
- free to be a 'normal' family
- free to have time to see the wider family and build relationships
- free to be me - full of lightness and laughter, rather than heavy with pain.

Holding all these sticky notes in my hand, I knelt on the floor and confessed my shortcomings to God. Then lifting up my hands I surrendered all my demands to Him, reading out the notes one by one and laying them down on the floor - I was transferring to God ownership of my own life and Julia's. 'Our lives are Yours,' I sobbed, 'do with them what You will.'

5. RECOGNISE THE IMPORTANCE OF PERSEVERING

The song, *Things can only get better* became well-known in the late 1990s after the Labour Party used it for their 1997 election campaign. Politicians of every party are always telling us that it's true; unfortunately it's not! Things don't always just get better – but the kingdom of God grows in hope. So it's important that we persevere in coming to terms with our disappointments – it's a process that has to be worked through. Perseverance is not necessarily one long race; it can be several short races one after another.

James, probably the brother of Jesus, teaches us that there is a higher principle involved when we encounter trials, suffering or disappointment. That higher principle is God's unchanging desire for our growth and maturity. At the beginning of his letter to early Christians, James speaks like this about perseverance: 'Consider it pure joy, my brothers and sisters, whenever you face trials of many kinds, because you know that the testing of your faith produces perseverance. Let perseverance finish its work so that you may be mature and complete, not lacking anything' (James 1:2–4).

We persevere with our struggles, with our emotional pain, with our relationship with our heavenly Father, and with our faith. Faith is about looking beyond our circumstances to the person of the Lord Jesus Christ. Do we want to be the kind of people who can watch every cherished dream go up in flames and yet still yearn to be intimately involved with our heavenly Father, still willing to take another risk because it delights His heart for us to do so? If we can persevere with this – and it takes real perseverance – we will find that living amid shattered dreams, dashed hopes and the consequent disappointment will enable us to catch a glimpse of a new dream emerging from the old one. Chris Ledger's daughter, Julia, wrote this poem, expressing her feelings about clinging on to God:

Hanging On
Lord, I'm hanging on to the edge of a cliff top,
Another push and I'll fall;
I'm at the end of my tether; I'll lose my grip
With any more pain, no matter how small.

I know You'll never test me beyond my endurance,
You'll lift me up onto level ground,
But I'm tired from dangling here so long,
My strength is fast running out.

Lord, give me patience in waiting,
Your comfort in the depths of my pain;
A reassuring word to hang on to
And grace to bear each hour, each day.

Lord, I thank You for the dangling on the cliff top
For it's in our dangling that we learn
To cling desperately onto You and rely
On Your perfect timing and Your master plan.

REFLECTION

We know that we are not intended to 'go it alone' as Christians – we need one another. A useful analogy might be this: we are an orchestra, with each person being a different instrument, which, when 'in tune' with one another, make up a harmonious whole. In Romans, Paul suggests another picture – that of a living sacrifice:

> Therefore, I urge you, brothers and sisters, in view of God's mercy, to offer your bodies as a living sacrifice, holy and pleasing to God – this is your true and proper worship. Do not conform to the pattern of this world, but be transformed by the renewing of your mind. Then you will be able to test and approve what God's will is – his good, pleasing and perfect will.
> (Rom. 12:1–2).

ACTIVITY

Prayerfully consider the two pictures given in the two quotations above – that of being part of an orchestra, and that of the 'living sacrifice', which Paul identifies as 'true and proper worship'. Which picture do you find most helpful and most relevant to your present circumstances? Ask God what He wants to show you as you think about these pictures. In God's presence we have no need to pretend about anything at all, because God sees us and knows us as we really are – and He still loves and accepts us. We cannot surprise or shock God!

PRAYERS

Lord, help me today to live my life as a tuneful act of worship to You; help me to remember that I'm part of an orchestra, that I'm not going it alone. Give me grace to follow the music written for me today and to keep my eyes on the conductor so that I stay in time with You and Your plans for me. Amen.

OR:

Father, may I live transformed today; renew my mind; renew my thoughts; give me the will, the perseverance and the grace to offer everything I do as a living sacrifice to You. Enable me to live in a way that brings glory to You, my Lord and my God. Amen.

CHAPTER SIX

HOPE AVENUE

We have journeyed now from that Lay By into which we pulled to assess the impact that our disappointment – whatever it may be – has had on us, and the damage it has caused in so many areas of our lives. We've travelled through Despair Street, trying to make sense of the confusion we were experiencing. We've held tight on the Bumpy Track, learning more about our feelings and negative thoughts and ways to manage them; we've learnt to trust God and surrender through Struggle Lane and now we find ourselves climbing up Hope Avenue.

PERSEVERING IN HOPE

Sometimes as we travel, thoughts about hope are beyond us because we are overwhelmed and frustrated with the disappointment. It's easy to lose sight of Paul's words:

> we rejoice in the hope of the glory of God. Not only so, but we
> also rejoice in our sufferings, because we know that suffering

produces perseverance; perseverance, character; and character, hope. And *hope does not disappoint us, because God has poured out his love into our hearts* by the Holy Spirit whom he has given us. (Rom. 5:2–5, NIV 1984, emphasis added)

As we look back at the way we've come so far, we may well ask ourselves, 'How am I to find a new hope after my experience of dashed hopes – an experience that God could have prevented? How do I trust a God who answers my prayers at a simple level, eg, "Help me to get a parking place as I'm running late", yet apparently disregards my prayer that my sister's treatment will shrink her inoperable brain tumour?'

We may never understand why we suffer. Christian hope is learning to place a growing confidence in God, who does not fail us. Hope and perseverance work together to help us through. Don't try to generate hope – ask for it! 'May the God of hope fill you with all joy and peace as you trust in him, so that you may overflow with hope by the power of the Holy Spirit' (Rom. 15:13). God doesn't do half-measures; He gives us more than enough to sustain us and carry us through.

If we are to discover an enduring hope, a hope that will continue through our ongoing struggles with disappointments – because there *will* be other disappointments – then such a hope will have certain characteristics:

- Such a hope is available to sick people, lonely people, disregarded and marginalised people, and it must be the same hope that is offered to those who are well, healthy, popular and rich.
- Such a hope thrives even when dreams shatter, sickness advances, poverty worsens, loneliness deepens and obscurity continues.

Where are we to find such a hope? The Bible has the answer! Yet the biblical idea conveyed by the word 'hope' is very different from the way you and I might use the word in everyday conversation.

THE MEANING OF HOPE IN THE BIBLE

The New International Version of the Bible, which is the one used chiefly in this book, has no fewer than 174 references to hope: ninety-four in the Old Testament and eighty in the New Testament. Just a handful of those use the word hope in the way we use it today, but most of them refer specifically to what the Bible means by 'hope'. In our day-to-day usage, I may look out of the window and say, 'I hope it's not going to rain because I've just hung out all my washing on the line to dry.' Or I may glance anxiously at my watch and say, 'I hope the bus arrives soon; I don't want to miss my train.' These senses of the word 'hope' suggest a rather vague wish that something will or will not happen. The biblical sense of hope is not like that at all. It's something very clear and definite. It's not a wishy-washy desire that something *may* happen, but a confident expectation that something *will* happen!

This is because hope, as the word is used in the Bible, is dependent on God's promises – and God's promises are absolutely certain. Our God is faithful to His word and to us. If God has promised something, He will do it. Our hope, as Christians, is inextricably linked to God's promises, most of which have already been fulfilled – Abraham hoped for the son God had promised him, even when Sarah, his wife, was well past the age of childbearing. His faith and hope were rewarded and the race of Israel was born. The Israelites, wandering in the wilderness, hoped for the promised land most of them didn't enter, because of their unbelief and wilful disobedience, but their children did. The Jews, exiled in Babylon, clung to the hope offered by the prophets that one day God would bring them back to their own land, because He had promised to do so. That hope was fulfilled. And all the time, throughout their very chequered history, the Israelites for hundreds of years were hoping to see the fulfilment of the greatest of God's promises – that a Redeemer and Deliverer would arise to set them free and to usher in a new age. That promise and that hope were both fulfilled in the Lord Jesus Christ. Today, our hope as Christians lies in the '"coming" he promised' (2 Pet. 3:4) and the assurance that whatever happens to us, God's grace is sufficient.

Hope in its biblical sense is very robust and active; it's linked to God's promises and the blessings we receive as we trust Christ for salvation. 'Hope is not a pussycat but a tiger, which can go for the jugular of sadness and despair,' as Ken Costa, churchwarden of Holy Trinity Brompton, said in a sermon in 2003. Biblical hope changes everything – the way we see ourselves, the way we live, our values and goals. This hope gives us a sense of purpose, an underlying sense of peace whatever we're going through, and a confidence in the God who loves us and values us individually.

Such a hope anchors us to God in the bad times, when we are left with shattered dreams and disappointments, as well as the good times, the times when our dreams come true and our longings materialise. In his first epistle the apostle Peter puts it like this:

> Praise be to the God and Father of our Lord Jesus Christ! In his great mercy he has given us new birth into a living hope through the resurrection of Jesus Christ from the dead, and into an inheritance that can never perish, spoil or fade.
>
> (1 Pet. 1:3–4)

God's raising of the Lord Jesus Christ from the dead set God's seal of approval on what Jesus achieved on the cross. As we enter into new life through Jesus we are born into a 'living hope', one that, unlike our earthly dreams and hopes, 'can never perish, spoil or fade away'. No wonder Peter is excited and full of praise to God!

The writer to the Hebrews has this to say about the hope that God offers us in Christ:

> We have this hope as *an anchor for the soul*, firm and secure. It enters the inner sanctuary behind the curtain, where our forerunner, Jesus, has entered on our behalf.
>
> (Heb. 6:19–20, emphasis added)

Some of you may be familiar with an old hymn, *Will your anchor hold in the storms of life*, which has these words as its chorus:

> We have an anchor that keeps the soul
> Steadfast and sure while the billows roll;
> Fastened to the Rock which cannot move,
> Grounded firm and deep in the Saviour's love.
> (Priscilla Jane Owens, 1882)

A modern paraphrase (*The Message*) of Hebrews 6:19 puts it this way: 'grab the promised hope with both hands and never let go.

It's an unbreakable spiritual lifeline'.

Hope is found in God's promises

God cannot lie, as the previous verse to the one mentioned above in Hebrews 6 reminds us: 'God did this so that, by two unchangeable things in which it is impossible for God to lie, we who have fled to take hold of the hope set before us may be greatly encouraged' (Heb. 6:18). Because it is 'impossible for God to lie', His promises are utterly trustworthy. So, paradoxically, shattered dreams and disappointments can be blessings because they can help us to discover the source of our true hope. God's promises are the springboard of our hope and our guarantee that even ultimately death, the greatest destruction of hope, will not prevail. Our ultimate hope, of course, is heaven, which is all very well, you may say, but what about the here and now? What is our hope for today?

Our hope for today stems from a trust that enables us to know that God is with us to strengthen us, to give us His peace and to comfort us in our shattered dreams and disappointments. 'God has said, "Never will I leave you; never will I forsake you"' (Heb. 13:5). However, we have to learn to be patient in our hope – many of the New Testament references to hope also refer to patience! There is often a time of waiting and that waiting can give rise to confusion. We need to remember the struggle Jesus had in the Garden of Gethsemane as He wrestled with the awful prospect of going to the cross for us, the disappointment He must have felt on a human level at that time, the dashed hope that His Father would allow 'this cup' (of intense suffering) to be taken from Him. Yet with the resurrection, God's power burst forth into the world, opening Hope Avenue to us.

94

GOD - THE DOOR OF HOPE

> Therefore I am now going to allure her; I will lead her into the
> wilderness and speak tenderly to her. There I will give her back her
> vineyards, and will make the Valley of Achor a door of hope. There
> she will respond as in the days of her youth
> (Hosea 2:14–15)

This verse from the book of Hosea needs a little background
information to make sense. It's a reference to a disastrous defeat
in battle at Ai that the Israelites, under Joshua's leadership,
suffered almost immediately after their conquest of the walled
city of Jericho. Jericho was the city that they had to destroy to
begin their conquest of the promised land, and the subsequent
defeat at Ai was a direct consequence of one man's disobedience
at Jericho. The Israelite army was instructed that everything was
to be destroyed, apart from precious metals which were to be put
into the Lord's house (Josh. 6:24).

However, one man, Achan, couldn't resist temptation: he
kept for himself 'a beautiful robe from Babylonia, two hundred
shekels of silver and a bar of gold weighing fifty shekels' (Josh.
7:21). Shortly afterwards the Israelites were routed by the men of
Ai, in what should have been an easily won battle.

Joshua and the elders of Israel were greatly dismayed at this –
not just because the battle had been lost but because God's name
had thus been dishonoured; they sought God's face in grief and
repentance and Achan, his family, his possessions and the stolen
goods were destroyed, at God's command, in the Valley of Achor.
The name 'Achor' (a variant of Achan) means something like
'trouble', so the valley where Achan died was called the Valley of

95

Trouble because of the trouble that Achan brought upon Israel as a result of his sin. From that point on 'Achor' or 'the valley of Achor' became a byword for trouble. Several centuries later the prophet Hosea spoke of the valley of Achor becoming a door of hope, secure in the knowledge that the allusion to Achor would be recognised by his listeners and readers.

Look again at Hosea's words and see how appropriate they are for us at this stage of the journey when we are travelling on Hope Avenue. The God who loves us as individuals, who knows what we've been through – the lost dreams, the dashed hopes and the disappointment that comes in their wake – this God can make our 'valley of Achor', the very valley of trial, trouble and disappointment, a doorway to new hope. Hosea speaks of God leading His beloved people into the wilderness – the place of barrenness and waste – and yet it's right there in that desolate place that God promises to 'speak tenderly'. Can you hear God speaking tenderly to you through your disappointment?

There is a similar idea in Isaiah where the prophet says: 'Break forth into joy, sing together, You waste places of Jerusalem! For the LORD has comforted His people' (Isa. 52:9, NKJV). Notice that it is the *waste places* – the barren, 'hope-less' places of our shattered dreams and disappointments – that are exhorted to break out in joy because 'the LORD has comforted His people'! God can make the waste places of our disappointments, our shattered dreams and lost hopes into places of fruitfulness and even joy.

Returning to the Hosea verses, we next see God's promise to restore, to give back vineyards – always a picture of growth and fruitfulness. Are you ready for God to restore your 'vineyard'? Our God is the God who can transform situations – even the most hopeless. He can turn our laments into the songs of our youth! If you can hold on to nothing else right now on your journey, hold on to this – God wants to make the valley of *your* trouble and disappointment into a doorway of hope for you. A doorway of the hope described in the Bible – a sure and certain hope, founded on and grounded in God's unbreakable, faithful promises; with a promise of growth and fruitfulness for good measure!

This sounds fine, you may be thinking, but just how do we go about this?

CHOOSING HOPE

> We must accept finite disappointment, but never lose infinite hope.
> (Martin Luther King, Jr.)

Hope is a choice we can make! The pain of disappointment is all too real, but sometimes we can become too comfortable with the pain, which acts like a 'comfort blanket', so that we dismiss the prospect of any hope. God promises that we will not experience the pain of disappointment and despair forever. Nowhere in Scripture is disappointment belittled. Instead it is recognised as a desire for something better: 'weeping may stay for the night, but rejoicing comes in the morning' (Psa. 30:5); 'Those who sow in tears will reap with songs of joy' (Psa. 126:5).

Choose to be rooted in the 'who' – the sovereignty of God – and not in the 'why'

When we become Christians, we surrender our lives to God. He is Lord of our lives; He knows what He is doing with us and He longs for us to trust Him wholeheartedly amidst the pain and disappointment; the lost hopes and shattered dreams. Rarely do we understand what God is doing in a time of disappointment. Sometimes as we look back later we can see what He was doing and how He worked things out for us according to His own good purposes, but often we don't understand and we won't until we reach heaven. It's important to gaze on and wonder at God's goodness, to worship Him for His promises and His greatness, to praise Him for all that is past and trust Him for all that's to come. God may not answer our anguished 'Why?' this side of eternity but that doesn't negate the fact that we can draw closer to Him through the pain. God would say to each of us, 'I am the WHO, let go of the WHY.'

Choose to surrender your life
'You are not your own; you were bought at a price' (1 Cor. 6:19–20). Let's remember that we are not autonomous: God owns us – we don't own ourselves and we deserve nothing from Him. Jesus paid a huge price for us in His death on the cross. Let's acknowledge this as often as we need to do so; whenever we feel our hearts becoming bitter, because bitterness destroys us from the inside out and will affect our relationship with God and with others. (See Chris Ledger's testimony in the previous chapter about surrendering her 'rights'.)

Choose to be rooted in faith and not in feelings
Faith enables us to be rooted in the unshakeable belief that God loves us (as demonstrated by Jesus on the cross). Faith begins and ends with trusting God's Word and His promises. Chris Ledger says, 'I found the best and most

helpful thing was to declare Scripture – not to argue, but to declare God's truth.'

Choose to use the Scriptures, songs and hymns to support and build your faith

As Chris Ledger says, declaring God's Word helps us to be rooted in our faith. Sometimes, especially when we are exhausted physically and emotionally, it helps to go back to familiar Bible verses or to sing (out loud or in our heads) hymns and songs that have blessed us in the past. The Psalms are a good source!

One of the most encouraging things about the book of Psalms is that the contents are so real and down to earth. Yes, there are glorious promises and wonderful hymns of praise to God for His creation, His power; His majesty. However, against these we have many amazingly honest and heartfelt cries to God from people in deep pain, people reeling from disappointment, shattered by disloyalty in those they had trusted, cries for help from people in fear of their lives. These are songs and laments rooted in experience, not imagination. The tears are genuine, the pain is raw; the disappointment and shattered dreams are only too real. Three in ten of the Psalms are laments – outpourings of grief to God – so you are in good company if that's where you turn when words of your own fail you and you need to cry out to God.

God is not easily offended and He can bear our anguished questions, 'How long, Lord?' and 'Why?' The freedom to complain to God was a feature of Israel's relationship with Him. Without it, there was always a danger that worship would be less than genuine – people saying or singing one thing but thinking and feeling another, which God hates. Lament is best understood as 'complaining with confidence' – admitting to God how we really feel (He knows anyway!) because we are confident He will hear our prayer.

'But I cry to you for help, LORD; in the morning my prayer comes before you. Why, LORD, do you reject me and hide your face from me?' (Psa. 88:13–14). If we are honest, there are times when we have all felt like that! Walter Brueggemann (Professor of Old Testament, Columbia University, USA) in a commendation of a book called *The Cry of the Soul* says this:

> Allender and Longman add an important contribution to a new wave of Psalm studies. There is an enormous temptation for 'high faith' to deny the 'dark side' of life where 'things do not work'. Against that ... they show how the Psalms make contact with the 'emotions of failure'. Such places in life become, by their sensitive reading of the Psalms, places of revelatory healing and transformation.[1]

The Israelites sang their songs of lament as worshipfully as they sang their songs of praise. Let's not hold back from 'lamenting' to God – telling Him honestly how hurt/sad/angry/desperate we feel. We seem to be as afraid of lamenting as we are of catching the flu! Openness and honesty provide the soil out of which can grow true confidence and joy.

REFLECTION
We have mentioned anchors in this chapter, in commenting on the verse from Hebrews, which speaks of Christian hope as an anchor for the soul. Let's just remind ourselves what an anchor does. It's a vital piece of equipment on a ship or boat

and its purpose is to stop the boat drifting or capsizing. The heavy, iron anchor is thrown overboard or lowered on the end of a long chain and settles into the seabed, sometimes hooking itself onto a rock or something similar. It thus prevents the ship from moving and stabilises it whilst it's not travelling.

There's a story about some inexperienced sailors who were unsure what to do about anchoring their boat when a hurricane was approaching. An older, experienced mariner advised them that their only hope was to 'anchor deep' and pray. Earlier we mentioned the old hymn whose chorus speaks of 'an anchor that keeps the soul steadfast and sure while the billows roll'. We can probably think of many 'spiritual anchors' but a few stand out:

- The love of God: we can be 'grounded firm and deep in the Saviour's love' as that hymn's chorus puts it. God's love in Christ is eternal and unchanging: 'his compassions never fail. They are new every morning' (Lam. 3:22–23). God's love and grace are inexhaustible.
- The peace of God: that peace that 'transcends all understanding' (Phil. 4:7) can anchor our souls when the storms of disappointment are raging.
- The Bible: God's written Word points us to His living Word – the Lord Jesus Christ. In Romans 15:4 the apostle Paul speaks of the 'Scriptures and the encouragement they provide' giving us 'hope'. God's Word is reliable, unshakeable and its promises will be brought to fruition, because they are based on God's unchanging character.

ACTIVITY

There is a saying that goes: 'Feed your faith and your doubts will starve.' What are the promises in God's Word that give you hope? Write out two or three verses that can feed your faith and be anchors for your soul. Keep the list somewhere where you can look at it easily and be encouraged to 'choose hope'.

PRAYER

'Show me your ways, LORD, teach me your paths. Guide me in your truth and teach me, for you are God my Saviour, and my hope is in you all day long … May integrity and uprightness protect me, because my hope, LORD, is in you.' Amen. (Psa. 25:4–5,21).

[1]Dr D. B. Allender and Dr T. Longman III, *The Cry of the Soul* (Colorado Springs: NavPress, 1994)

AFTERWORD

Open Highway: A new dream, a new beginning
In the first chapter of this book we used the example of Naomi to illustrate the fact that as we trust God through our disappointments, lost dreams and shattered hopes, those very experiences can open the door to new dreams and new beginnings. With God it's never 'the end'.

The writer of Ruth intends us to see Naomi at the end of the story as a deeply contented old woman, aware that sometimes God has a higher purpose for our lives than merely for things to go well from a human perspective. In her old age, Naomi experienced a joy that more than replaced the happiness she had lost. God had indeed, through Ruth and Boaz, given her 'beauty instead of ashes, the oil of joy instead of mourning, and a garment of praise instead of a spirit of despair' (Isa. 61:3).

If Naomi could speak to us now what might she say? I think she might well report, 'Everything worked out for the best. It was hard, but don't let pain cause you to miss the potential of shattered dreams to change your life, for good, forever.'

You've come through the disappointment journey – the Lay By, where, your expectations shattered, you sit in shock and disbelief and assess the damage, then the descent into Despair Street asking, 'Why, God?' and a myriad of other questions. After that you've experienced a very Bumpy Track with your chaotic emotions and your thoughts. That Bumpy Track leads eventually to Struggle Lane where you learned the importance of relinquishment and surrender before climbing the hill of Hope Avenue … but that's not the end. At the end of Hope Avenue is the Open Highway – the road to the future, to a new dream and a new beginning with your hand in the hand of your loving heavenly Father.

Our prayer is that you will be given grace to walk with God, away from the shattered dreams, lost hopes and disappointment; into God's new dream, His loving plan and purpose for the rest of your life.

RESOURCES

Further reading

For further reading on some of the issues raised in Chapter 4, The Bumpy Track, we recommend the following:

C. Blake and C. Ledger, *Insight into Anxiety* (Farnham: CWR, 2011)

C. Ledger and W. Bray, *Insight into Depression* (Farnham: CWR, 2009)

W. Bray and C. Ledger, *Insight into Anger* (Farnham: CWR, 2007)

R. Kallmier and S. Jacobs, *Insight into Forgiveness* (Farnham: CWR, 2008)

For further reading on the subject of disappointment and illness, we recommend:

C. Ledger, *Shattered Dreams: A Mother's Pain* (Gloucestershire: Word for Life Trust, 2002)

Counselling

CWR offers an Advice and Counselling Referrals Service. Contact Jennifer Jones on 01344 893107. (If you are unable to reach Jennifer, please leave a message and she will return your call at her earliest convenience.) Please note: this is a landline number and charged at standard network rates but the Advice Counselling Referrals Service is free. Counsellors, who callers are referred to, do charge an hourly rate, but there is no obligation to use their services.

The Association of Christian Counsellors has a list of counsellors and counselling organisations across the country. Go to **www.acc-uk.org** for details.

APPENDIX

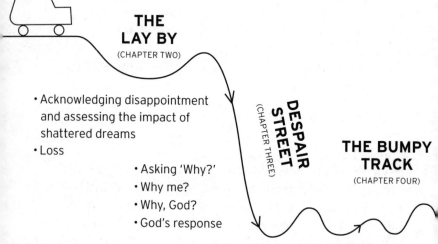

THE LAY BY
(CHAPTER TWO)

DESPAIR STREET
(CHAPTER THREE)

THE BUMPY TRACK
(CHAPTER FOUR)

• Acknowledging disappointment
  and assessing the impact of
  shattered dreams
• Loss

  • Asking 'Why?'
  • Why me?
  • Why, God?
  • God's response

• The five areas affected by unm
  expectations and desires
• The bumps on the track

**OPEN
HIGHWAY**
(AFTERWORD)

HOPE AVENUE
(CHAPTER SIX)

STRUGGLE LANE
(CHAPTER FIVE)

- Persevering in hope
- The meaning of hope
  in the Bible
- God – the door of hope
- Choosing hope

Recognise and acknowledge your struggle

Recognise that Jesus is with you

Recognise whether you are trusting God and what

you are trusting God *for*

Recognise the importance of relinquishment:

surrendering our hopes and dreams

Recognise the importance of persevering

Insight series

Handling issues that are feared, ignored or misunderstood.

The *Waverley Abbey Insight Series* is based on one-day seminars held by CWR at Waverley Abbey House to give insight into key issues with which many people struggle today.

Explore our full range of Insight books, courses and pamphlets.

BOOKS

Insight into Anxiety
by Clare Blake and Chris Ledger
ISBN: 978-1-85345-662-6

Insight into Self-Esteem
by Chris Ledger and Wendy Bray
ISBN: 978-1-85345-663-3

Insight into Depression
by Chris Ledger and Wendy Bray
ISBN: 978-1-85345-538-4

Insight into Stress
by Beverley Shepherd
ISBN: 978-1-85345-790-6

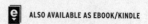 **ALSO AVAILABLE AS EBOOK/KINDLE**

For a complete list of the 17 titles available in this series visit
www.cwr.org.uk/insight
Available online or from Christian bookshops.

COURSES

These invaluable teaching days are designed both for those who would like to come for their own benefit and for those who seek to support people facing particular issues.

For the latest course information and dates about CWR's one-day Insight seminars visit
www.cwr.org.uk/insightdays

PAMPHLETS

These short guides offer help in understanding and addressing problems effectively. They come in packs of 10 so you can always keep them handy to give to sufferers or their friends/relatives.

Waverley Abbey Insight Pamphlet – Stress
ISBN: 978-1-85345-608-4

Waverley Abbey Insight Pamphlet – Depression
ISBN: 978-1-85345-609-1

Waverley Abbey Insight Pamphlet – Self-Esteem
ISBN: 978-1-85345-637-4

Waverley Abbey Insight Pamphlet – Anxiety
ISBN: 978-1-85345-641-1

Available online or from Christian bookshops.

Courses and seminars

Waverley Abbey College

Publishing and media

Conference facilities

Transforming lives

CWR's vision is to enable people to experience personal transformation through applying God's Word to their lives and relationships.

Our Bible-based training and resources help people around the world to:
• Grow in their walk with God
• Understand and apply Scripture to their lives
• Resource themselves and their church
• Develop pastoral care and counselling skills
• Train for leadership
• Strengthen relationships, marriage and family life and much more.

Our insightful writers provide daily Bible-reading notes and other resources for all ages, and our experienced course designers and presenters have gained an international reputation for excellence and effectiveness.

CWR's Training and Conference Centres in Surrey and East Sussex, England, provide excellent facilities in idyllic settings – ideal for both learning and spiritual refreshment.

CWR Applying God's Word
to everyday life and relationships

CWR, Waverley Abbey House,
Waverley Lane, Farnham,
Surrey GU9 8EP, UK

Telephone: +44 (0)1252 784700
Email: info@cwr.org.uk
Website: www.cwr.org.uk

Registered Charity No 294387
Company Registration No 1990308